Praise for *MBA D*

'This book is one to read in a week and refer to for a career. It provides the models and theories to use, and inspires leaders to build stable and visionary organisations. I felt like a door had been held open for me into a world of ideas and experience that will help me in my management and leadership.'

Jo Youle, CEO and Founder, Missing People

'In an age where the relevance of an MBA is being questioned, Chris's book justifies why we need MBAs. This is my go-to book. Whether preparing for a module, undertaking an assignment or considering my next steps at work, I turn to this book as my North Star.'

Lt Col Chris Lane MBE RA, British Army

'*MBA Day by Day* is the most read book on my bookshelf; there's not been a week gone by that I haven't referred back to it. It's so good I've bought copies for friends and colleagues thinking about their own career development.'

Frankie Cory, CEO, Mischief PR

'Not simply just another management book, *MBA Day by Day* offers a comprehensive overview of an MBA written in a highly readable manner. Whether an experienced or aspiring manager, this book will stimulate and challenge thought processes, encouraging the reader to stop and reflect about work and life.'

Roberta Pace Balzan, Brand Manager, Roche UK

'A fantastic resource for any manager looking to broaden their scope and understanding of how an organisation works. *MBA Day by Day* proved the importance of personal reflection in holding myself accountable in my role.'

Chantelle van der Merwe, retail industry consultant, South Africa

'A great introduction to the key topics covered in an MBA and also a good recap for senior leaders. I ask all my colleagues to read this book before considering starting an MBA.'

Jouni Riuttanen, Sales Director, Etteplan Oyj, Finland

'This book was my go-to resource for a simple, digestible overview of concepts throughout my MBA, and subsequently as I put my learning into practice in my work. A concise guide that demystifies and shows the links between disparate subjects, I heartily endorse *MBA Day by Day* to anyone who seeks to understand the subject matter of an MBA.'

Edwin Geuter, Chief Strategy Officer, Right Stone

'This book provides unbelievably helpful and easy to digest content that simplifies an otherwise complicated process.'

Ryan Matthew Lukas, Creative Director, Hi-Tek Signs & Designs

MBA Day by Day

Pearson

At Pearson, we have a simple mission: to help people make more of their lives through learning.

We combine innovative learning technology with trusted content and educational expertise to provide engaging and effective learning experiences that serve people wherever and whenever they are learning.

From classroom to boardroom, our curriculum materials, digital learning tools and testing programmes help to educate millions of people worldwide – more than any other private enterprise.

Every day our work helps learning flourish, and wherever learning flourishes, so do people.

To learn more, please visit us at **www.pearson.com/uk**

MBA Day by Day

How to turn world-class
business thinking into everyday
business brilliance

Second edition

Chris Dalton, PhD

Pearson

Harlow, England • London • New York • Boston • San Francisco • Toronto • Sydney
Dubai • Singapore • Hong Kong • Tokyo • Seoul • Taipei • New Delhi
Cape Town • São Paulo • Mexico City • Madrid • Amsterdam • Munich • Paris • Milan

PEARSON EDUCATION LIMITED
KAO Two
KAO Park
Harlow CM17 9SR
United Kingdom
Tel: +44 (0)1279 623623
Web: www.pearson.com/uk

First published 2015 (print and electronic)
Second edition published 2019 (print and electronic)

© Chris Dalton 2015 (print and electronic)
© Pearson Education Limited 2019 (print and electronic)

The right of Chris Dalton to be identified as author of this work has been
asserted by him in accordance with the Copyright, Designs and Patents
Act 1988.

Pearson Education is not responsible for the content of third-party internet sites.

ISBN: 978-1-292-28681-5 (print)
       978-1-292-28682-2 (PDF)
       978-1-292-28683-9 (ePub)

British Library Cataloguing-in-Publication Data
A catalogue record for the print edition is available from the British Library

Library of Congress Cataloging-in-Publication Data
A catalog record for the print edition is available from the Library of Congress

10 9 8 7 6 5 4 3 2 1
23 22 21 20 19

Cover design by Two Associates
Front cover image © Dacian_G/iStock/Getty Images

Print edition typeset in Melior Com 9pt by SPi Global
Printed by Ashford Colour Press Ltd, Gosport

NOTE THAT ANY PAGE CROSS REFERENCES REFER TO THE PRINT EDITION

Contents

List of figures

Publisher's acknowledgements

004 Dow Jones & Company, Inc: Henry Mintzberg, quoted in http://online.wsj.com/news/articles/SB10001424052970204908604574334450179298822 **007 Martino Publishing:** Fayol, H. and Storrs, C. (2013) General and Industrial Management, Martino Fine Books. **017 John Wiley & Sons:** Box, G. and Draper, N. (1987) Empirical Model Building and Response Surfaces, John Wiley & Sons. **021 Ralph Waldo Emerson:** Ralph Waldo Emerson **023 Alan Watts:** Alan Watts **024 John Wiley & Sons:** Schön, D.A. (1983) The Reflective Practitioner: How professionals think in action, Jossey-Bass. **031 Norton & Co. Ltd:** Adapted by the author from Erikson, E. (1994) Identity and the Life Cycle, W.W. Norton & Co. Ltd. Reproduced with permission. **036 CIPD Publishing:** Hardingham, A. (2004) The Coach's Coach: Personal development for personal developers, Chartered Institute of Personnel and Development. **044 Lewis Carroll:** Lewis Carroll, Alice in Wonderland **047 Crown Copyright:** Adapted from "Valued care in mental health: Improving for excellence" (2018), NHS Improvement. https://improvement. nhs.uk/resources/valued-care-mental-health-improving-excellence/ **063 Jean-Paul Sartre:** Jean-Paul Sartre **076 Sage Publications:** Adapted from Rousseau, D.M. (1995) Psychological Contracts in Organizations: Understanding written and unwritten agreements, Sage Publications, Inc. Reproduced with permission. **077 David Beeney:** David Beeney **080 John Wiley & Sons:** Lencioni, P. (2002) The Five Dysfunctions of a Team: A leadership fable, John Wiley & Sons. **082 Taylor & Francis:** Belbin, M. (2010)

Team Roles at Work, 2nd Edition, Routledge **086 CIPD:**
Purcell, J., Kinnie, N., Hutchinson, S., Rayton, B. and
Swart, J. (2003) 'Understanding the People and Performance
Link: Unlocking the Black Box', with the permission of
the Chartered Institute of Personnel and Development.
London (www.cipd.co.uk). **089 Woody Allen:** Woody Allen
103 Wm Morrison Supermarkets PLC: www.morrisons-
corporate.com **105 Wm Morrison Supermarkets PLC:** www.
morrisons-corporate.com **107 Wm Morrison Supermarkets
PLC:** www.morrisons-corporate.com **117 Peter Drucker:**
Peter Drucker **119 CIM:** www.cim.co.uk/files/7ps.pdf **123
Emerald Group Publishing Limited:** Payne, A., Ballantyne,
D. and Christopher, M. (2005) 'A stakeholder approach
to relationship marketing strategy: The development and
use of the "six markets' model"', European Journal of
Marketing, 39(7/8): 855–871. Reproduced with permission
of Emerald Group Publishing Ltd. **129 Pearson Education:**
Kotler, P. et al. (2012) Marketing Management, European
Edition, Pearson, p. 574. **133 Harvard Business School:**
Fombrun, C.J. (1996) Reputation: Realizing value from the
corporate image, Harvard Business School Press. **138 Sun
Tzu:** Sun Tzu **139 Macmillan Publishers:** Drucker, P. (1979)
Management, Pan Books, p. 445. **144 Simon & Schuster:**
Porter, M.E. (2004) Competitive Strategy: Techniques for
analyzing industries and competitors, New Edition, Free
Press. **144 The Institute of Management Sciences:** Mintzberg,
H. (1978) 'Patterns in strategy formation', Management
Science, 24(9): 934–948. **155 Academy of Management:**
Mitchell, R., Agle, B. and Wood, D. (1997) 'Toward a theory
of stakeholder identification and salience: Defining the
principle of who and what really counts', The Academy
of Management Review, 22(4): 853–886. Reproduced with
permission of The Academy of Management. **161 Donald J.
Trump:** Donald J. Trump (CNN Republican debate, 16/9/15)
179 Penguin Books: The Wealth of Nations by Adam
Smith (1982), **180 Lewis Carrol:** Lewis Carrol, Alice in

Wonderland (1865) **182 Fortune Media IP Limited:** Fortune Global 500, 2018 Fortune.com/global500/att/ **202 Arthur Schopenhauer:** Arthur Schopenhauer **209 Gulf Publishing Co:** Adapted from Blake, R. and Mouton, J. (1985) The Managerial Grid III: The key to leadership excellence, Gulf Publishing Co. Reproduced with permission. **212 Seven Star Communications:** Tzu, L. (1989) The Complete Works of Lao Tzu, Seven Star Communications. **214 Paulist Press International:** Greenleaf, R. and Spears, L. (2002) Servant Leadership: A journey into the nature of legitimate power and greatness, 25th Anniversary Edition, Paulist Press International. **218 Peter Anderton:** Peter Anderton **220 Kotter International:** http://www.kotterinternational.com/our-principles/changesteps/changesteps, Kotter International. Reproduced with permission. **223 Guy Kawasaki:** Guy Kawasaki quoted from 2015 article on Mashable.com https://mashable.com/2015/05/05/guy-kawasaki-apple-watch/#xhwVNRBynaqj **228 Rafael dos Santos:** Rafael dos Santos **241 Ray C Anderson:** Ray C Anderson, founder of Interface Inc. **243 World Economic Forum:** https://www.weforum.org/reports/the-global-risks-report-2018 **246 The New York Times Company:** Milton Friedman, 'The social responsibility of business is to increase its profits', The New York Times Magazine, 13 September 1970. © The New York Times Company. **245 Elsevier:** Adapted from Carroll, A.B. (1991) 'The pyramid of corporate social responsibility: Toward the moral management of organizational stakeholders', Business Horizons, 34(4): 39–48. Reproduced with permission of Elsevier. **250 Oxford University Press:** World Commission on Environment and Development (1987) Our Common Future, Oxford University Press. **251 United Nations:** Glossary of Environment Statistics, Studies in Methods, Series F, No. 67, United Nations, New York, 1997. **255 Ray Anderson's:** Ray Anderson's **262 Penguin Random House:** Brook, P. (2008) The Empty Space, Penguin Modern Classics. **264 William Shakespeare:** Shakespeare **271 Penguin**

Random House: Marcus Aurelius (2006), Meditations, Penguin Classics **271 China Publishing & Media:** Zhu Xi, (1986), Zhuxi yulei [Classified Dialogues of Master Zhu], Li Jingde (ed.), Beijing: Zhonghua shuju **278 Elsevier:** Jay, J.K. and Johnson K.L. (2002) 'Capturing complexity: A typology of reflective practice for teacher education', Teaching and Teacher Education, 18(1): 73–85.

About the author

I have over 27 years of experience in management education and training. I work at Henley Business School, at the University of Reading in the UK, where I am Associate Professor of Management Learning. My specialist area is Personal Development and I teach MBA workshops, run corporate development and lead seminars related to management development in many parts of the world. In the past, I have been Director for the Henley Distance Learning (Flexible) MBA, a programme with more than 3,000 executives worldwide, and Director of the full-time and modular MBA programmes at the Central European University Business School in Budapest, Hungary. I'm passionate about the power of reflection in management education. I hold a PhD in Management Learning and Leadership from Lancaster University and an MBA from Henley.

Preface

The scope of the subject matter of *MBA Day by Day* presents a real limitation for a book, namely that there will always be more ideas than pages available. Not everything can fit, and perhaps not everything should, and I ask forgiveness in advance for any omission that the reader feels important. I believe I can defend the claim that what is included is a good oversight of the essentials of MBA practice and thinking.

This book appeared first as *The Every Day MBA* in 2015 and I welcome the opportunity of updating both content and cases. Much of Part 4 (Visionary MBA thinking) has been restructured to reflect the importance of change in management and learning, and there is a new chapter on entrepreneurship. I'd like to thank my editor at Pearson, Eloise Cook, and my colleagues at Henley Business School for their wisdom and advice. In particular, I owe a debt to Professor Carole Print for her guidance in the finance chapters, to students and alumni of the Henley Executive MBA for their support and feedback, and to Diana Naya for inspiration in the last chapter.

About this book

After reading this book, you will:

✓ understand key concepts, theories and models of an MBA
✓ be ready to apply new ways of thinking to your job
✓ be able to hold informed conversations with colleagues with MBAs
✓ reflect on, re-evaluate and improve your performance
✓ realise that you knew more than you thought, and ...
✓ begin to appreciate how much more there is to know! Learning is a life-long process.

This book is for:

▌ aspiring/new managers and managers with great experience but no MBA
▌ anyone interested in accelerating their career in business or management
▌ managers who already have an MBA but want to refresh or continue their development
▌ learning and development leaders in any organisation that value MBA thinking and behaviours
▌ educators and trainers who want to understand how MBAs think.

Introduction

Welcome to *MBA Day by Day*. This book is a guide to applying world-class MBA principles and thinking at work.

Whether you have ambitions to do an MBA or already have one, in business and management those three letters certainly seem to exert quite a hold over the imagination. Every year, tens of thousands of managers around the world invest their time, energy and money to graduate with a master's degree in business administration. No book can equal that achievement or capture everything that years of study contain. It can, however, highlight two things that graduates from top business schools have discovered:

1. The most lasting benefit of an MBA is a change in your thinking.

2. Informed self-awareness is the key to new behaviours, better decision making and continuing career growth.

Presumably, managers already think, otherwise their actions would just be automatic. So, what is so special about the change in thinking brought about by an MBA? One answer could be simply that MBA thinking accelerates promotion to the next level. True, but a more powerful idea is that the best MBAs are people educated to see a special relationship between thinking and action that can make a real difference to achievement at work, one's career and the impact of business on a changing world. Using clear and concise language, this book will use the typical structure and experience of an MBA to challenge you to apply ideas and new ways of thinking about what you do.

Key points about *MBA Day by Day*

Each chapter covers a crucial area of management and leadership featured in MBA study. You will find overviews of concepts, key models, frameworks and theories, as well as real-world illustrations. You will be encouraged to practise the types of thinking developed in the top programmes around the world.

Three assumptions underpin *MBA Day by Day* and I want you to keep them in mind as you work through the book.

1 An MBA links practice and theory

Academic rigour mixed with practical, industry-specific knowledge of the kind that you develop simply by doing your job is a powerful equation. MBAs are good at combining these different kinds of knowledge. True, the more experience of the workplace you have, the more you can get from this book but, if you are at an early point in your career, you will also find many ways to apply MBA thinking to the lessons that the first few years of management always bring.

2 An MBA challenges deep-set habits

What is required and rewarded early in a management career is not necessarily what is required or suitable at more senior levels. Success at entry and middle levels needs certain skills, but some of these habits can become barriers later in your career. Many of our habits are deep-set and are often taken for granted. They are difficult to spot and even harder to change or let go. An MBA is all about such personal development.

3 An MBA addresses what it really takes to become a senior manager or leader

Business is now a global phenomenon. In only the last 50 years, the world has changed beyond recognition and no doubt it will be transformed again completely in the coming half century. Business schools are no better or worse at predicting the future than the rest of society, but they are great places to develop the critical and reflective thinking abilities required to work in uncertainty and change. It is not about what you learn, it is about knowing how you learn, how you think and how you act as a leader. With awareness and dedication, you can begin to prepare yourself for leadership roles now.

Structure of the book

MBA Day by Day is organised in four parts.

Part 1 (Chapters 1–2) is about management, MBAs and you, and how to apply this book. Like many at the start of an actual MBA, you may be tempted to skip the first section and jump to the 'real stuff' in Part 2. Try to resist this because self-awareness and good preparation are key to learning. Before you start to read about the various parts of management practice, you need to invest some time becoming aware of yourself and your experience. Personal development is knowing how to reflect on practice so that you can see immediate results as well as preparing for the future.

Part 2 (Chapters 3–5) is about tactical thinking in the management of a firm's resources. We examine the core subject areas of the first phase of an MBA, highlighting commonly used models and insightful theories. Each part links to one of the types of thinking used by an MBA, and you will be able to follow suggestions to apply these to your management practice.

Part 3 (Chapters 6–9) moves on to strategic thinking and concerns the internal and external environment of organisations. This part of the MBA brings to the fore the idea of managing relationships, including the ones an organisation has with its customers and its competitors, as well as the complex task of understanding the rapidly changing nature of international business.

Part 4 (Chapters 10–13) looks at visionary thinking in leadership and management. By visionary, I mean the special kind of future-focused pattern recognition that both flows from and informs tactical and strategic thinking. All the chapters in this part are about change. Here we look at leadership, entrepreneurship and the pressing subject of sustainability. The final chapter offers some advice for self-awareness and meeting the challenges of management and career.

Look out for plenty of suggestions in *Day by Day practice* activities and *Questions for reflection* throughout the book. Again, you may be tempted to skip these, but they are essential because such tasks get you exploring what you and others do in your organisation. They may well challenge some of your core ***assumptions***. In addition, at the end of each chapter, there are suggestions for further reading and extra questions that will help your personal development.

A *glossary* containing management and MBA thinking concepts appears at the end. In the text, glossary entries are ***bold italics*** when they first appear.

1

part

MBA Day By Day: making it work for you

Reflection n. [rɪˈflɛkʃ(ə)n]: serious thought and consideration

M anagement is a practical activity and the key to being a better manager lies in thoughtful action, day by day. The key to thoughtful action lies in self-awareness. Learning about yourself never stops because reality never stops being your teacher. However, life can be your teacher only if you are awake to it and, in this respect, the majority of managers are asleep. Management training is not enough because it is about behaviour modification, not self-awareness. The aim of management training is to create dependency for answers on the trainer. Consequently, organisations invest time and money in staff development and meet only limited success. Management education is about awareness. The aim of management education is for you to free yourself from restraints to your thinking. There are thousands of business schools but, believe it or not, there is no hard evidence that the MBA *curriculum* makes better decision making. Good business schools are amazing places, and what these schools know is that, while content is important, education is about creating the right conditions to develop managerial identity and purpose. Here are four things you can do to get the most out of reading *MBA Day by Day*:

1   **Start getting to know yourself.** Keep a notebook with you at all times (without lines, if possible, to get you out of the habit of thinking in lists). Have plenty of pens and pencils to write with. Writing down your thoughts and your observations becomes a sort of conversation with yourself.

2   **Engage your brain.** Our brains are amazing and they work through association, so start connecting to new ideas using the same principles your mind functions with. Learn how to draw a mind map (visit Tony Buzan's website **www.thinkbuzan.com** if you are not already familiar with this tool).

3 *Consciously* **decide to be curious.** Be an explorer. Open, non-judgemental curiosity is essential to creativity. Catch yourself whenever you say 'Yes, *but* ...' and replace that with 'Yes, *and* ...' and see the difference it makes.

4 **Find some starting points for comparison.** Rate yourself for each of the following and indicate whether you think you are below, at or above average.[1]

	I'm below average	I'm average	I'm above average
My IQ			
My skill as a manager			
My skill as a leader			
My analytical skills			
My critical thinking skills			
My self-awareness			
My interpersonal skills			
My creativity			

Now, you're ready to go.

Note

1 Research shows that potential employers are mostly looking for the last four, not the first four.

Management and the MBA
Your business needs you!

> *The great myth is the manager as orchestra conductor. It's this idea of standing on a pedestal and you wave your baton and accounting comes in, and you wave it somewhere else and marketing chimes in with accounting, and they all sound very glorious. But management is more like orchestra conducting during rehearsals, when everything is going wrong.*
>
> Henry Mintzberg, quoted in the *Wall Street Journal*, 2009[1]

In a nutshell

The need for skilled managers has never been greater and, globally, the number of people in management is set to grow in the coming decades. The MBA reigns supreme as the badge of quality in business administration, yet only 1 in every 200 managers will get to do one. A business degree is a great thing, but you don't need one to start thinking about purpose and contribution to the bottom line. With discipline and curiosity, you can make huge strides in your professional life.

In this chapter you will:

▌ learn about the history and main functions of management

▌ define the purpose of management

▐ discover the structure and goals of the MBA

▐ write your first reflections and do your first activities for your daily management practice

Why this book?

There may be many reasons why you have decided to read this book. Perhaps you are new to management and are feeling a bit overwhelmed. Equally, you could have plenty of experience but feel stuck in your career, as though you have reached a plateau. You may have a long list of specialist qualifications under your belt and are now beginning to think about an MBA as the next step. Or maybe you don't have formal education behind you, have improvised from day one and somehow fear being exposed for this (by the way, this is known as the *imposter syndrome* and is a lot more common in management than you might think). Alternatively, you may just be curious about business and education in general, or incredibly busy and feel that, if you were better informed, you would have a little more control over your career path.

Whatever your story, there will be something in *MBA Day by Day* from which you can benefit. But, to find out what that is, you will need to do some critical thinking and some reflective writing as you go. So, before anything else, here are your first tasks.

QUESTIONS FOR REFLECTION

1 Why did you pick up this book?

2 What is your management style? How would a colleague describe you?

As you go through the book, I want you to develop the habit of regularly making such notes – this is one of the things that will lead you to reflective practice (more on this in

Chapter 2) and, in Parts 2, 3 and 4, you will find a couple of reflection questions at the end of each chapter.

An open mindset is the only route to insights from this book. Critical practice – that is, doing it with your eyes wide open – is a key facet of an MBA, so you will also see regular suggestions for things to apply or ideas to investigate in your own job. Here is the first.

DAY BY DAY PRACTICE

1 Make a list of at least three *assumptions* you've made about management. State the obvious. The more basic, the better.

2 Now think about your organisation. List another three things you take for granted or would never question about the place where you work. Look for things that 'need no explanation'. Discuss your lists with friends or work colleagues.

Assumption naming is an important thinking skill and not an easy one, but by the end of this book you should be able to see that each assumption you identified in the activity above sits on another that is more basic. And, even if you rated yourself as 'above average' in critical thinking skills in the list I gave earlier, you may struggle to name all your own assumptions in your day-to-day activities as a manager. Carrying out these reflective tasks is part of training yourself to challenge how you see the world.

Management

Since this is a book about management and the MBA, we should start by understanding what these terms mean.

Having a job is nothing new, but the domain of management is a relatively modern notion. It has roots in the industrial revolution more than 200 years ago, so its meaning was forged in an era of corporate invention, mass production, division of labour and admiration for the methods of science. Industrialised societies have benefited from unparalleled advances in technology, improvements in public health and social welfare, establishment of global trade, and high standards of education. Yet, they have also seen exponential growth in human population, unquestioning exploitation of natural resources, destructive armed conflicts at every level from local to global, and repeated cycles of economic boom and bust. For better or worse, there can be little doubt that today business shapes and misshapes our world.

There has never been a shortage of thinkers to make sense of all of this. In 1916, French mining engineer Henri Fayol published a **seminal** text on management.[2] It contained six functions of management that have proved quite resilient:

1. Forecasting and planning
2. Organising
3. Commanding or directing
4. Coordinating
5. Developing outputs
6. Controlling (through feedback)

Fayol's views were echoed by others. For example, US engineer Frederick W. Taylor championed management as a precise science of time and motion. 'Taylorism' belongs to a classical view of management built around **technical rationality** and though it may now seem outdated, many organisations still owe something to it. The Ford Motor Company applied it to assembly-line production and Total Quality Management (TQM) united, for a time, organisational hierarchy and supply chain in every department, as Six Sigma attempts to do today.

The most influential voice shaping our understanding of the organisation of business in the second half of the twentieth century was Peter Drucker, who wrote extensively on the role of management in a wide variety of settings. Drucker made a number of accurate predictions and coined many terms, such as 'knowledge worker', 'outsourcing' and 'management by objective'. One of the reasons his work remains important is his consistent belief that management is a matter of hierarchy *and* relationship.

Do these views still hold true today? Well, yes, and no.

Yes, in that we often rely on the past to show us the way to the future. Organisations, like people, derive a sense of identity from what has gone before and there are many turning points from the past that, for better or worse, still matter in management thinking. Consider just three:

▋ In 1888, a US court held that a private corporation was entitled to the same constitutional protection in law as a US citizen, and the concept of 'corporate personhood' was born. The results? First, a population explosion of businesses that are born (and die) every year around the world. Second, we are now comfortable thinking of organisations as if they have minds, identities, rights and ambitions entirely of their own. Third, huge diversity in what these corporate persons do, but almost no disparity in how they are organised (that is, they all tend to have the same basic structure).

▋ From 1927 to 1932, Elton Mayo conducted a series of experiments at Western Electric's Hawthorne plant in Chicago. A good management scientist, his original aim had been research on how the company's lighting products could boost productivity on any manufacturing shop-floor. In trying to test for this, he unintentionally found that productivity under experimental conditions increased, no matter what variable was changed. At the time, no one made the connection with the context of an experiment itself. Little significance was seen in the social aspect of the study until the 1950s when, in a new era of behavioural psychology, others revisited those results and concluded that productivity had improved because supervisors and staff paid attention to each other. The 'Hawthorne effect' was coined and the **human relations movement** was born.

▌In the late 1950s, the Gordon and Howell report (in the UK)[3] and the Ford and Carnegie Foundation report (in the USA)[4] strongly advocated the use of principles and practices from management science in the education of managers at business schools. Universities invested heavily in their business schools, the management disciplines took shape and the MBA took off.

This legacy still influences how your organisation is set up and these and other landmark moments have shaped management. But they are not the whole story. Management is constantly shifting and its definition is broad. Like all science, it will continue to evolve, but there is still no single, over-arching 'theory' of management.

When economic times are hard, management is often blamed. Many (including some insiders) have accused business schools of being part of the problem, not the solution. Renowned Indian academic Sumantra Ghoshal warned against MBAs relying too much on the 'gloomy' economic theory of greed and self-interest dominating business.[5] Ghoshal believed that the job of senior management was not to change people but to change the context so that those people could flourish. Canadian strategy guru Henry Mintzberg has appealed to MBAs to use more thoughtful reflection on experience in the classroom.[6] There are, indeed, many issues in today's business environment that call for new thinking, such as the following:

▌An existential threat to our environment through the effects of human activity. Population growth, resource depletion

and climate change are challenging many taken-for-granted
assumptions about our economic model and fundamentally
challenging the business world to be part of a solution, not
the problem.

❚ The rapid and accelerating changes being brought about by
new technologies and by efforts to understand the uses and
abuses of large amounts of data. There is a global shift towards
artificial intelligence and an incorporation of networked
computer systems into production, distribution and research.
Accumulating knowledge is no longer power. Power now
comes from how you access and share ***information***.

❚ The world of work is changing. Managing or leading others
is no longer about authority and positions of power in
a hierarchy but rather your self-awareness and skills in
connecting all the resources around you.

QUESTIONS FOR REFLECTION

1 What do you think the role of management in business is?

2 How is management defined in the organisation for
which you work?

The purpose of management: value creation

Management is a proxy activity. Someone has to stand in
for founders or shareholders when an organisation becomes
too big for those people to handle on their own. Therefore,
fundamentally, a manager represents the interests of others;
they cannot do entirely what they please. Another word for
this interest is value. Management must create value and,
wherever you are in an organisation, you need to understand
what is meant by this.

Value traditionally is measured in business by money (e.g.
by economic profit, which we cover in Chapter 5) but it

can, and should, also be measured in other ways. Although profit margin is one measure, there are other metrics that can measure value, such as a care for what your customers are getting from the relationship, how suppliers are in tune with your internal processes or the extent to which your fellow employees are contributing to those processes.

When it comes down to it, the world wants managers who can:

- make decisions under uncertainty
- gather, process and analyse information quickly and thoroughly
- communicate effectively on paper and face to face
- see the strategic connection inherent in every situation.

To get all these things done, especially in larger organisations, the role of management is often layered into first, middle and senior.

First-level managers have three main tasks:

- **Learning from doing:** gaining hands-on experience of the subject matter in their part of the organisation is the best way to pick up basic knowledge skills. This is on-the-job training with some leeway given to learn from mistakes.

- **Learning the ropes:** behind all the processes and systems lies the culture of the organisation – this is the 'how we do things round here' part, and is how it *actually* works. Over time, the new manager will pick up habits and shortcuts that minimise the need for trial and error.

- **Taking on responsibility and decision making:** completing relatively basic management tasks such as meeting agreed targets or mastering limited staff supervision and development. The politics of the organisation are rarely an obstacle at this level because there is little that you can do (usually ...) to rock the boat.

Middle managers have all these – plus three more:

▋ **An informed curiosity:** a hunger for new knowledge and for new ways of doing the job better.

▋ **Self-preservation:** the practical necessity to align with senior management's definition of value creation. This is a big one. Managers are constrained in what they can and can't do and must weigh up day-to-day decision making between what subject knowledge and experience tell them and what politics will allow or condone.

▋ **Responsibility for implementing small- to medium-scale change:** middle management is mostly a process of adjusting what is already there, as opposed to creating new things from scratch. Middle managers rarely get the chance for visionary leadership.

Middle management is the engine room for many organisations, but is the most exhausting level to be in. Effective middle managers may be given the chance, eventually, to lead at the top and, as senior managers, they get three additional tasks:

▋ **Stand in place of the founder or owners:** their task is, above all else, to decide what will maximise rather than destroy value for the shareholders of a business. This is despite the owners being only one category of stakeholder, and value being measurable in many other ways.

▋ **Translate the vision and set the strategy:** ultimately, they are responsible not just for the direction but also for the consequences of everybody's actions.

▋ **Keep eyes and ears open:** continuously survey and interact with the external environment and prepare for the future context.

Truly successful organisations are those that create an environment of possibility, trust and openness, where middle managers can reach their full potential as they create value for stakeholders. That, however, is rarely the case. Few people work harder than middle managers because they are the bridge between day-to-day operational tasks and the big picture, but in organisations with a confused context at the senior management level their efforts can end in frustration and burn-out.

The good news is that the MBA is very relevant to the tasks of middle management and is preparation for the complexities and challenges of senior management and leadership. This is exciting. With the right ingredients, MBA thinking can be life-changing.

QUESTIONS FOR REFLECTION

1. Which level of management do you work in? What tells you this?
2. How do you feel within this organisation? Make some notes under the following headings: long-term commitment, material rewards, current emotional state, professional pride.

In summary, management involves:

- acting with thoughtful purpose and intention
- being the symbolic but active representative of the owners of a business or organisation
- consciously using resources to create value in a way that is socially and ethically acceptable
- setting the context for future performance.

The MBA

We've discussed what management is, now we'll look in a bit more detail at the MBA degree.

The MBA is a generalist degree. It was first offered at Harvard in 1908, but management remained stubbornly vocational for several decades after that. In fact, the MBA did not gain much acceptance until the 1950s when shifts in education policy and economic growth following the Second World War combined to create demand for qualified practitioners. It has not looked back. In the United States alone, more than 250,000 people are currently studying for an MBA, offered to them by nearly 1,000 institutions. The MBA now accounts for nearly two-thirds of all graduate business degrees. If you want to do an MBA in the United States, there are plenty of schools to choose from, but expect a two-year full-time course and an average age among your fellow (largely non-US) classmates of 28.

In Europe, where the MBA arrived in 1957 at INSEAD in France and in 1964 at London Business School, the market is dominated by part-time study and the average age is a lot higher. In emerging economies, the degree is rapidly growing as a mass-market product by big business schools in large universities. Class sizes in full-time MBAs may vary from a handful to several hundred, depending on the school. MBAs are expensive. Fees on many MBAs are high and usually don't include living costs or the opportunity cost of a year or two away from employment. Nearly everywhere, men still outnumber women in most MBA classes, as they do in the boardroom – something that business schools ought to be changing (some are).

The cliché of an MBA is an ambitious, power-hungry and brash male manager investing in a year or two off work, eager to show their competitive zeal and mental agility, and equally eager to trample over their colleagues to finish top of the class and get hired by a leading consultant or bank. There may be some people like that but, actually, it's not representative of the majority of students, who are professionals with management experience and fewer expectations that the return on their study will be measured only in salary and bonuses.

Why does anyone do an MBA?

Management is a process of both personal identity and analytical sense making. An MBA involves a lot of work in what is already the busiest period of a person's working life. Reading, writing assignments and exams, classroom discussions and group work, myriad adjustments in work–life balance and major changes in perspective and beliefs – all are typical of the experience. An MBA is about understanding and then managing changes in the web of relationships between senior and middle levels of management. The value of doing one comes from the applicability of your learning to a range of industries, in a host of situations, across a world of cultural divides. An MBA will not make you a genius in every field, but it ought to equip you to manage, lead and inspire others who *are* experts in theirs. This requires good character, astute self-awareness and strong thinking skills.

So, why doesn't everyone do one? The majority of managers in the world will never do an MBA, and not just because there are many more managers than spaces. It's expensive, it consumes time that most people never seem to have in the first place, and it imbalances further the precarious mix of work, family, relationships and other parts of your life. On top of that, there is nothing magic about a business school other than creating the right context for personal development. However, with determination and support, you can achieve many of the same results through self-awareness and application to self-study.

MBA thinking: why is it so important?

The goal of management training is to change or add behaviours and create dependency on the trainer. The goal of management education is to open the mind and eyes and create freedom from the educator. As we saw in the introduction, this book is about MBA thinking, or thinking like an MBA day by day. So, let's be clear and precise about thinking, because how you think is part of creating value.

We use the word 'thinking' in a number of ways. It can mean the background 'streams' of conscious and semi-conscious images and ideas that pass through our minds, usually unchallenged, every day. We don't have to conjure them – thoughts just come and go. Equally, it can mean the deliberate mental process linking enquiry/explanation to reasoning/action. Largely, it is the second one of these that is MBA thinking, and it can be learnt (but don't forget about the importance of the first). As you read on, keep in mind two important facts about thinking:

1 Thinking is our way of dividing up a 'messy' world into categories so that we can agree how to act for the best. If a category doesn't correspond to the way the world is, you will end up in trouble.

2 We all have the ability to think about our thinking. This is a skill we can develop.

What are concepts, frameworks, models and theories?

People who do an MBA often get a boost to self-confidence early on because new vocabulary and concepts picked up on the course can make a huge difference to how they feel and how others see them; application and feedback are immediate. The MBA has its own grammar, so it will help to highlight a few important terms now:

Concepts: our way of making complexity manageable is by naming parts. A concept, or construct, is a name we give to an idea and is very handy for working with each other. Concepts are used together to build maps of ideas. Business contains a bewildering number of concepts (e.g. profit, competitive advantage, culture, etc.) and these form the vocabulary of management.

Frameworks: representations, often visual, of concepts that have something in common. A good framework is useful because it organises your thinking in a structured way. The concepts in a framework are not connected in a particular sequence, and you could start anywhere.

Models: with a model, it *does* matter where you start and in which order the concepts are placed because there is a relationship between them (e.g. cause and effect). Models are shortcuts. MBAs, academics and business practitioners like them because they store wisdom and quickly let you apply other people's thinking to a given problem or question. There is a difference, however, between a model 'of'' something and a model 'for' it. The former is descriptive and our best guess, the latter is prescriptive and a 'how to' guide. Occasionally, MBA models are both. Finally, the statistician George Box once said, 'Essentially, all models are wrong, but some are useful', so keep this in mind.[7]

Theories: our current best explanations for how we think the world works. Good theories aim to explain as wide a set of phenomena as possible and provide a basis for testing predictions. A better theory is one that explains more than its predecessor. Theories are there to help make sense of incoming information and are fine-tuned by trying to find their limits. MBAs are not attracted to theory usually until it's too late! Theory building is driven by curiosity.

The three phases of a typical MBA programme

Imagine you were creating an MBA curriculum, where would you begin? With strategy? Leadership? Personal development? Study skills? Team building? Or would you launch into one of the functional modules? All these approaches exist, but most programmes conform to three conventions:

1. Separate business and management into subjects.
2. Group subjects into parts/stages.
3. Sequence stages, usually from simple to complex, functional to strategic, and core to elective.

This feels linear, and it is. You might also feel that this does not map exactly onto the messy world as you experience it at work, and it doesn't. But it is a way to organise a lot of ideas and content while you develop your reflective thinking skills as a manager. I want to make *MBA Day by Day* useful for those at work and those studying, so the book will follow roughly the same pattern.

The thinking skills that the MBA develops can be seen to have three phases:

Phase 1 – Tactical: using facts gained from experience to help make managerial decisions, taking action in line with existing strategy, networking, looking for incremental improvements, 'problem solving'.

Phase 2 – Strategic: using context, developing a relational view of situations, participating in strategy formation, communicating and implementing strategy, 'problem setting'.

Phase 3 – Visionary: asking 'what could be?', being an independent learner, critical thinker, systematic questioner of assumptions and asker of unsettling questions, becoming an effective leader, 'problem dissolving'.

Because an MBA is about personal growth, running alongside these is a fourth type of thinking: *reflective*. It is, arguably, the most vital, but also the one that many MBA students – and MBA programmes – neglect.

DAY BY DAY PRACTICE

1 Talk to at least one person who is in a senior role in your organisation and find out how they got into management.

2 What type of thinking (tactical, strategic or visionary) does your current job require from you most?

For most people, the career journey is experienced as parts that add up, step by step, to a whole. To be given greater responsibility in management first means proving you are competent at making decisions, solving problems and directing the work of others. In important ways, things do change when you become responsible for more. Your decisions are bigger, fewer in number, based on a broader range of considerations and much less reversible.

Putting it together: always learning

At the end of each chapter, I will encourage you to think about how that part of the book fits into the bigger picture.

Often, we say that we know what a manager is by combining what a manager does with what a manager thinks and knows. Everything you do as a manager happens in relation to everything else and management is, by its nature, always interconnected. Each chapter in *MBA Day by Day* is a new perspective on the same thing. Before we consider those separate points of view, I want you to consider how much you know about the person you are.

Further reading

A classic text:	*HBR's 10 Must Reads: The essentials* (2011), Harvard Business Review Press. A collection of seminal articles in *HBR* by the 'big guns' of management thinking.
Going deeper:	*A Very Short, Fairly Interesting and Reasonably Cheap Book About Studying Organizations* by Chris Grey (2012), Sage Books. I really recommend this book, though it is a challenging read in some parts.

Understanding Organizations by Charles Handy (4th edition 1993), Penguin. A respected figure in management thinking and practice, Handy's book imaginatively shows how real people are what make organisations work.

Watch this: 'Confessions of a micromanager' – Chieh Huang's 2018 TED talk in which the Silicon Valley entrepreneur shares some lessons about management as his company grew: **https://www.ted.com/ talks/chieh_huang_confessions_of_a_ recovering_micromanager/up-next**.

Notes

1 https://www.wsj.com/articles/SB10001424052970204908604574334450179298822.

2 Fayol, H. and Storrs, C. (2013) *General and Industrial Management*, Martino Fine Books.

3 Gordon, R.A. and Howell, J.E. (1959) *Higher Education for Business*, Columbia University Press.

4 Canning, R.J., Robert, I.D. *et al.* (1961) 'Report of the Committee on the Study of the Ford and Carnegie Foundation Reports', *Accounting Review*, American Accounting Association, 191.

5 Ghoshal, S. (2005) 'Bad management theories are destroying good management practices', *Academy of Management Learning & Education*, 4(1): 75–91.

6 Mintzberg, H. (2004) *Managers, Not MBAs: A Hard Look at the Soft Practice of Managing and Management Development*, Berrett-Koehler Publishers.

7 Box, G. and Draper, N. (1987) *Empirical Model Building and Response Surfaces*, John Wiley & Sons.

You and your personal development
Lifelong learning is a necessity, not a luxury

> *What lies behind us and what lies before us are tiny matters compared to what lies within.*
>
> Ralph Waldo Emerson

In a nutshell

Good MBA programmes rely on students who are both bright and self-aware and I have the same philosophy for this book. I will ask you to reflect on your work and life experience and be honest about what you know and what you don't know (including what you pretend not to know) about yourself. This is part of personal development but it is also linked to having management impact in an organisation.

In this chapter you will:

▌ define reflection and reflective practice

▌ think about different aspects of your personality

▌ look at your strengths and focus on setting development goals

▌ begin to think about your purpose

The keys to personal development

This chapter is unashamedly about you. Health and well-being are what sustain worldly success, but many of us have this the wrong way around. Before you go further, write down your answers to these questions for reflection.

> **QUESTIONS FOR REFLECTION**
>
> **1** When was the last time you were able to stop, think and reflect on your career? Thinking and action go together; what did you do next?
>
> **2** We don't usually think about what's important in life until we face a crisis or a serious dilemma. Write some notes about:
>
> (a) the highest point in your life so far and
>
> (b) the lowest point.

'Know thyself' is an ancient instruction. It is both a call for introspective honesty and humility and a means to know where you belong in society. Personal development involves both your internal and external worlds. Self-awareness is the starting point for learning, so being aware of your personal values, beliefs, capabilities and motivations is a route to emotional maturity in your thinking. I define personal development as:

> the identification and removal of those restraints that limit the likelihood of sustainable individual, organisational, social and environmental health and well-being.

This is a bit of a mouthful, but the main message is about health and well-being at every level. When I begin a personal development journey with a group of MBAs, I want them to do four things:

1 Understand the concepts of reflection and reflective practice.

2 Adopt a mindset of curiosity.

3 Use this curiosity to ask questions.

4 Get into the habit of writing things down.

Taken together, these are a route to action. Time is precious. You're busy and may believe you can't afford to stop and think about what you do. I think that's why you can't afford not to.

Reflection and reflective practice

If you are a mid-career manager, you're probably already too busy to think, let alone reflect. Most managers know **reflection**, if they know it at all, as part of a problem-solving process. Something goes wrong; time is spent collectively or alone reviewing what happened in the hope that identifying the cause will improve the process. But this is limited – reflection is much more than that. So, before we go on, here are some truths about reflection:

- It is always about 'unfinished business'; the stuff that refuses to be parked or buried.

- You can't reflect on something if you haven't noticed it, and reflection is about discovering what is still absent after you have got that far.

- There are many ways to reflect and not all of them are comfortable. You will sometimes feel vulnerable.

- The point of reflection is, in the end, to get unstuck. As British philosopher Alan Watts once said, 'We are on a journey to where we are', and I think this is what reflection does for us.

Managers sometimes use reflection as a *technical* tool to work out what went wrong in order to fix it (as, for example, in a 'lessons learned' or project wash-up) and also as a more careful process of looking at what needs to change in order to *align* things to the overall goals of their organisation. Or, they may apply reflection *critically*, questioning all assumptions underneath an issue. This deeper reflection sometimes can be a response to a major change or trauma where your world has been turned upside down, but it can also be found in the mundane and ordinary.

We like to think of management as a highly ordered and predictable professional activity. But, if you think about how your normal working day in management actually goes, the chances are that you don't inhabit a Zen-like, unruffled state of expertise. Rather, you live in a world of constant interruption, surprise and frustration.

In his book *The Reflective Practitioner*, US academic Donald Schön noted that professionals who train for years in the neat and ordered world of theory actually do their jobs in the 'swampy lowlands' of everyday experience.[1] Management happens at the intersection of theory and practice, although most managers learn the skill of 'thinking on their feet' before they become experts in theory. Intuition will work for you up to a point, but becoming expert in identifying underlying assumptions (which often includes the power relations and politics of the office) requires something extra. Reflection is the most important way to think through all the wider concerns than simply the problem in hand.

Curiosity and self-awareness

If you want to apply what is in this book, your curiosity first needs to be woken up. Look back at your answers to the first couple of questions for reflection in Chapter 1. Was curiosity one of the reasons you picked up *MBA Day by Day*? Let's get curious now about four areas of personal development that MBAs often think of at the start of a programme:

Personality: Who am I? What is important to me?

Proficiency: What am I good at? What do I need to develop? What are my goals?

Purpose: What is my contribution to the world?

Practice: What action should I take? What's stopping me?

Let's look at each of these in turn.

Personality: Who am I?

'What makes me the way I am?' 'Is my character from nature or nurture?' 'Is my personality fixed, or can it be changed?' I have learned over the years, working alongside mature MBAs, that these are difficult questions to ask. In fact, the big one – 'Who am I?' – is never fully answered.

There are literally hundreds of tools, psychometric tests and questionnaires out there to test a host of theories about personality, and I'll list some below. I believe that personality tests can be useful, but they have limits because any test is only as good as the theory behind it. The vast diversity of questionnaires and models is actually based on only a few core theories of character and personality and the majority of tests are uncritical (and sometimes unaware) of the assumptions made by their underlying theory. One of the main ideas in this book is that you need to develop your ability to think critically, something that becomes more important the higher you get in management. For that reason, I think you should try to find as many ways as possible to investigate your personality.

Values, beliefs and psychometric tests

In every human civilisation, values address the 'why' of life and they define us as humans, giving rise to collective principles and individual beliefs that guide and give meaning to our actions. Beliefs and principles differ between people and can change and evolve over time, but values are universal and, at an elemental level, are not a matter of choice. Universal values relate to:

▌ *being productive* as a member of society

▌ *being moral* or *ethical* with others

▌ *belonging* to society, the collective or a group

▌ *being aware* of self.

Management education often treats these values as measurable and rationally worked out by individuals. A more holistic approach says that values are messy, intuitive and preverbal. Perhaps they are a bit of both.

Beliefs are the shortcuts we use to make choices in behaviours, what everybody else actually sees about us and on which they judge us. Beliefs are rules, not opinions. In fact, most of our beliefs are habitual and rarely questioned. They hold us in place and are the bridge between actions and values. If you want to learn and grow, you will need to identify which beliefs are self-limiting – and replace them. Most of us are very resistant to changing our beliefs because it risks changing our personality.

Psychometrics is the attempt to measure a person's personality or character. For nearly 100 years, individuals and organisations have used a range of psychometric questionnaires to assess personality and it's likely that you have come across several such instruments in your career. They work by converting a statistical analysis of your responses into a best-guess report on attitudes, aptitudes, traits, characteristics or preferences.

One type of psychometric test measures aptitudes, skills or preferences for behaviour. Understanding what you are good at (or not good at) is a starting point for improving your skills. This popular focus on strengths in management learning is part of the positive psychology movement, which says that you should find out what you are good at ... and do more of it. Tom Rath's best-selling book *StrengthsFinder 2.0* is an example of this concept.[2]

Behaviours and attitudes can change, but personality traits are more fixed. Not surprisingly, many of the tests for this aspect of personality were developed from the psychoanalytical tradition. They promise better-informed ways of understanding the self in relation to other types. The best known is the Myers–Briggs Type Indicator (MBTI), a US personality test loosely based on the work of Carl Jung. It is widely used to clarify orientation to the world across four dimensions through innate preferences in how you take in and process information. The 4 sets of preferences result in 16 personality types. MBTI is similar to the Keirsey Temperament Sorter (accessible online for free). The Five Factor Model uses the acronym OCEAN as a way of remembering what are also called the 'Big Five' personality traits: openness, conscientiousness, extraversion, agreeableness and neuroticism. The result is a very broad way of identifying self-reported traits with behaviours. In a similar way, measures of personal values and belief systems, such as Hogan's Motives, Values and Preferences Inventory (MVPI), encourage you to name your value set from a long list.

Any of these may be a good starting place to think about what's important for you, but psychometric test results are seductive, and it's worth remembering a couple of caveats so that you avoid the trap of pigeon-holing:

1. They are not magic. When you fill out a questionnaire about yourself, it's likely that it will tell you what you already know.

2. If the theory behind them is not correct, then the results will be of limited practical value for your personal development in the long run.

It's better to use test scores alongside a range of other sources of information and to discuss your thoughts with colleagues and friends in order to arrive at an informed view of yourself.

Proficiency: what am I good at?

The statistical measurement of mental intelligence was not proposed until the beginning of the twentieth century. Interest in IQ, or intelligence quotient, was fed by society's needs to find ways to assess and grade children in education and adults in work; a love of educational testing that has not diminished since. In recent years, the popularity of Daniel Goleman's work on *emotional intelligence* (EI) has also become durable. EI broadly covers self and social awareness, self-management and interpersonal skills and was inspired by Howard Gardner's theory of multiple intelligences. EI is now becoming mainstream for many in learning, and often is combined with growing interest in the neuroscience of learning. Advances in our understanding of what the brain does when we learn have enabled us to map some of the process involved, though this is not quite the same as explaining the meaning of personality.

Nevertheless, 'What am I good at?' is a fundamental question for every manager to ask.

QUESTIONS FOR REFLECTION

1 When you were young, what were you good at? What are you good at now?

2 At work, what are you rewarded for? What are you good at but not rewarded for in your work life?

Take a look at your answer to the first question above. Was it easy or difficult to come up with things in which you excel? What about weaknesses, are they important also? What criteria do you use to measure success?

The dominant indicator of personal effectiveness used by organisations is the concept of **competency**. Competencies are effective behaviours that drive outcomes. The idea is that, if certain skills can be developed, this will result in a high level of performance against the goals and targets set by your workplace. It may also be a sustainable advantage in the job market. In fact, competency-based practice is so widespread it would be difficult to find many companies that don't plan, measure and evaluate managerial performance this way. Making a link between skills, effective behaviours and outcomes is one way to find developmental gaps, but it is not the whole story (if only it were that simple). Not everything in management can be reduced to a measurable competency so easily.

If you are intending to get on in your career, explore new directions or even look for a way out, then a thorough re-evaluation of personality type and perception is a start. My experience with MBAs has shown me that a more thought-provoking question to ask is: Where are you in your life cycle? This is because the answer must involve you looking at yourself in relation to the world to understand your identity and purpose.

Purpose: what is my contribution?

Personal development is the process of advancing identity and self-knowledge, of developing talents, potential and employability across our lifespan. It involves us acknowledging where we are in the present, and sometimes letting go of things from our past. In Chapter 1, you were asked to reflect on why you had picked up this book. Did you identify a sense of challenge at work or a need to move on in your career? Would it have made sense for you to think about these things five or ten years ago? Why not leave it until later in your career? Why now?

DAY BY DAY PRACTICE

Life chapters

This is a great exercise to do in order to identify patterns in your life and, perhaps, signals of what to let go.

Imagine your life as if it were a book, with each stage or part its own chapter. First, try to draw a timeline to identify these stages and key events or turning points. Then, write a title and short summary for each chapter and include, if you can, transitions from one chapter to the next. Your 'book' is unfinished, but you may now be able to identify patterns and recurring themes.

What it means to be an adult is not a simple question. Danish-American psychiatrist Erik Erikson viewed life as a cycle from birth to death with eight stages of development. As we go through life, biology, cognitive development and – crucially – the social environment combine naturally to trigger various struggles. Erikson called them 'crises', which we must deal with in order to understand a particular core value. The best known of Erikson's psychosocial transitions is probably the 'identity crisis' of adolescence. Less well known are the three further stages of adulthood (see Figure 2.1). It is those adult periods that cover your career.

We leave adolescence and enter young adulthood, where our concern is learning what (and who) we care for. This is a formative period in our lives, one where we build relationships and families. Erikson believed that, from our mid-30s to our early 60s, we move to mature adulthood, where we are, inevitably, drawn outward to the question of our productivity and how we shape the world around us. At this stage, we face a crisis between 'generativity', or the extension of love into the future, and 'stagnation', which is this energy selfishly turned in to please only ourselves. Are we able to balance this societal role and this concern with how the world is for future generations and still leave time and space for ourselves? This is the personal context for management. If you can work through this, understanding both sides of the conflict, it can make it incredibly productive.

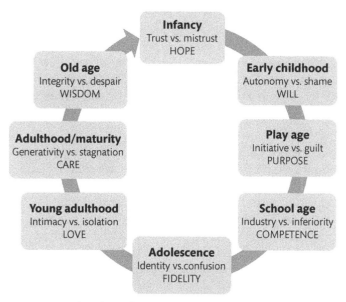

FIGURE 2.1 Erikson's psychosocial life cycle model of development
Source: Adapted by the author from Erikson, E. (1994) *Identity and the Life Cycle*, W.W. Norton & Co. Ltd. Reproduced with permission.

The power of contribution

In 2017 Rob Lynes had reached a crossroads in his career. Having studied linguistics at a British university, he had worked in a number of central European countries in the 1980s and 90s. In 1995 he joined the British Council, and his 23 years in that organisation had been hugely rewarding and successful. He had risen through the ranks amid a series of directorships in the Middle East, India and the UK, and deputy director of global operations. This had culminated in the award of Companion in the Order of St Michael and St George (CMG) in recognition for promoting UK-India cultural and educational ties.

With this under his belt, and with children now grown, Rob reached his 50s with all his energy and enthusiasm intact, but with a question mark as to what purpose it should be put. With his experience and credentials, a senior role in any one of a number of national or international organisations or advisory roles to others might be a logical next step. Instead Rob chose to take time out to think. This was not to be idle time, however.

'Throughout my life, I have always given a lot of value and thought to impact,' he says. 'I am now at a stage where impact is more important than ever. However, what has changed is the type of impact I want to make, and for what purpose. I look for opportunities where I feel my contribution can have a more direct positive impact on those I am working with, as well as the wider society. I want to be closer to this impact and to be able to see real tangible benefits to those that I am working directly with.'

In 2018, Rob committed to spending a year in India advising the leadership of Future Hope, a charity that provides housing, education and homes to some of the most vulnerable street children in Kolkata. 'The thing that drives and motivates me', says Rob, 'is the direct, positive social impact I can make personally from the work I do. In return, I feel a greater sense of satisfaction and meaning from seeing the impact this has on individuals.'

We all face some of these inner questions during this period of our lives, after we have met the challenges of the first phase of adulthood. It's easy to see how the life-cycle concept maps onto the challenges of moving from middle to senior management (you can compare this with Jim Collins' thoughts on leadership in Chapter 10).

DAY BY DAY PRACTICE

What are the three most important words or phrases in your life right now?

Write these down. Ask a significant person in your life to do the same and then informally compare and discuss the result.

Practice: what action should I take?

What are your goals? As we established in the previous chapter, management is a purposive activity; it has an end in mind. Goal setting at work is, therefore, not usually a problem. When it comes to the personal, a lot of people have a hunch that something needs to change but cannot accurately say what that is, and often set up goals that are too vague, not compelling or simply unmanageable. So, while it certainly helps to have developmental goals that are expressed in positive language, and for them to be measurable and precisely written out, only awareness of who and where you are right now is the essential part. You can then be flexible to new information as you go, which also brings you one step closer to understanding MBA thinking.

Visionary managers become leaders not because they have all the answers but because they know they don't. When you begin with a very keen understanding of the current situation and a strong urge to move things in a certain direction, goals emerge. Then so do the actions to reach them.

DAY BY DAY PRACTICE

1 Write down, in as much detail as you can:

   (a) one short-term work or career goal

   (b) one medium-term work or career goal

   (c) one long-term career goal.

2 Share and discuss these goals with another person. For each, also tell another person the first concrete action you will take towards each (telling someone else increases the likelihood of it happening).

How to get more balanced

Work–life balance is about having a say in when, where and how you work, and recognising that it is healthy to try to achieve a fulfilling life both inside and outside work. Having your view accepted and respected by others (organisations, families and society as a whole) is important in avoiding too much stress or burn-out. While there are no hard and fast rules about how a person should divide up their lives, most of us will recognise a few major categories such as health, levels of attainment at work or in our career, relationships with those closest to us, and an inner world of self-actualisation and purpose. Our lives are full of tensions, dilemmas and choices, both at work and at home.

A great way of seeing how things are balanced in your life is in a wheel of life, a diagnostic tool developed for **coaching**. Constructing your own wheel is a great way to identify and perhaps surprise yourself about where you need to put your energies. Figure 2.2 shows a blank version. You can recreate your own with labels such as 'physical environment', 'family and friends', 'career', 'money', 'health', 'recreation', 'significant other/spouse', 'spirituality', the choice is yours. To create your own wheel of life, first select eight aspects of

your life that are important to you and use each to label a
segment. Decide, on a scale of 1–10, how satisfied you are at
the moment with each. Then colour in your own chart and
(on your own or in conversation with someone else) identify
which one needs action now. It might not be the one with the
lowest score.

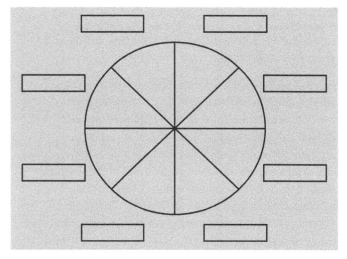

FIGURE 2.2 Blank version of the wheel of life

DAY BY DAY PRACTICE

1 Have a go at creating your own wheel of life (use
coloured pencils to shade in the different sections).

2 Do you have access to a professional or business coach
at work? What are the pros and cons of working with
one?

The wheel is one of the most versatile prompts for noticing
what's absent. You can even create variants that go deeper.
How about a 'wheel of personal goals', or 'wheel of stress', or

even a 'wheel of priorities'? No wonder coaches love using it with clients.

Coaching is still developing as a profession and is also now seen as a skill that managers need to have. Top executive coach Alison Hardingham, in her book *The Coach's Coach*, has this definition, as someone who:

> helps another person or group of people articulate and achieve their goals, through conversation with them. Coaching happens whenever that happens; and it happens all the time, not just in meetings with people who carry the title of 'coach'.[3]

Managers should not be in a formal coaching relationship with their subordinates, but a coaching mindset energises and refocuses and can be used in many different contexts. Managers often comment that their general approach to building and developing relationships improves as they coach and are coached by others. At the heart of the coaching is the ability to build rapport with another person. One useful framework for this is the GROW model developed by John Whitmore.[4] This is a structured process for setting and clarifying development goals:

Goal: dig or mine for topics and objectives that will challenge and engage you, and that will deliver real value for you, your organisation or the community you live in.

Identify two or three primary goals and add a 'shine' to each – shape each one with a wording that makes it feel real and exciting. Your goals should inspire you and they should produce an emotional response in you.

Reality: where are you now? What is the gap between this and where your goal sits? What is pushing you towards your goals? What is stopping you? Your reality changes all the time. As you move towards your goal, your reality moves as well.

Options: these are alternatives, choices. Not choices for alternative goals but choices on what actions you can take to move towards a given goal. Be as creative as you can.

Will: the final step is to commit to action. Any procrastination or lack of motivation should be noted (it may be there for a reason). The GROW model is not linear.

Finding tools to use in your career development

Early in your career there is a strong case for a competency-based view of skills acquisition and for using personality assessment tools in a methodical and measurable way. But experience has taught me that these are less useful the more you progress and the older you get. Your skills and competencies become more fluid with experience.

One good stepping stone between the two comes from Stephen Covey's book *The 7 Habits of Highly Effective People*.[5] This is a great set of questions to challenge yourself to take control of your personal development. Covey wants you to go from being dependent on others for your learning to independence (taking responsibility for yourself) through to interdependence (integrating with your context).

▌ **Habits 1 to 4:** going from dependence to independence:

- Be pro-active: take responsibility for your personal development.

- Begin with the end in mind: 'if you don't know where you are going, any road will take you there' is the saying.

- Put first things first: categorise tasks by importance, not urgency.

- Think win-win: seek solutions to problems that benefit others as well as yourself.

▌**Habits 5 to 7:** moving from independence to interdependence:

- Understand first, before trying to be understood: shut up and listen. You will learn from others.

- Synergise: creativity comes from combining ideas. Innovation is one of the emergent properties of this.

- Sharpen the saw: a mental attitude of constant improvement, life-long learning.

You need to shift focus from you just as a separate individual to you as an integrated part of a complex system. In 2004, Covey added an eighth habit – Find your voice and inspire others to find theirs.

DAY BY DAY PRACTICE

The world of work is constantly changing. Remote working has been an option for many knowledge workers for some time, but does it work for a whole company? Watch the TED talk 'Working from Home is Better for Business', by Matt Gullenweg, CEO and founder of *Automattic*, a distributed tech company with no offices.[6]

1 What do you think of their **business model**?

2 Do you agree with his conclusions?

3 Would distributed working help or hinder your organisation?

QUESTION FOR REFLECTION

1 How will the world of work change for you between now and retirement? (Will you even retire?)

2 You and your personal development

Putting it together: approaching management with an open mind

Management in the middle levels of organisations demands and rewards the efficient use of limited resources to meet short-term targets. Organisations will on the whole promote skills that solve problems and bring closure. This is stressful, if only because success and a changing world have a tendency to produce more work, not less. To be a better manager or leader you need breakthrough management practice, which requires the following:

1. Self-awareness, self-knowledge and reflective practice. This is not just a question of your strengths and weaknesses.

2. Understanding complexity and uncertainty in the business environment.

That is what MBA thinking develops. In the remainder of the book, we start to explore how this world operates. You will continue to be asked questions designed to improve your reflective practice. In addition, at the end of each chapter, there will be one or two personal development questions for you to consider.

Further reading

A classic text: *The 7 Habits of Highly Effective People* by Stephen Covey (2007), Simon & Schuster.

Going deeper: *Quiet: The Power of Introverts in a World That Can't Stop Talking* by Susan Cain (2013), Penguin Books. Cain's book is a refreshing examination of a side of leadership and management we often don't hear about.

Watch these: 'The Power of Vulnerability', Brené
Brown's relaxed TEDx talk, given
in 2013, which tells of her research
into stories of whole-heartedness,
strength and self-esteem in
vulnerability: **https://www.ted.com/talks/
brene_brown_on_vulnerability**.

Video extract of *psychiatrist Viktor
Frankl* being interviewed in 1977
about his beliefs about the search
for meaning: **www.youtube.com/
watch?v=YpN2D_tGsiY**.

Notes

1 Schön, D.A. (1983) *The Reflective Practitioner: How Professionals Think in Action*. Jossey-Bass.
2 Rath, T. (2007) *StrengthsFinder 2.0.*, Gallup Press.
3 Hardingham, A. (2004) *The Coach's Coach: Personal Development for Personal Developers*, Chartered Institute of Personnel and Development.
4 Whitmore, J. (2009) *Coaching for Performance: GROWing Human Potential and Purpose – The Principles and Practice of Coaching and Leadership*, 4th edition. Nicholas Brealey Publishing.
5 Covey, S. (2007) *The 7 Habits of Highly Effective People*. Simon & Schuster.
6 Facebook 'The Way We Work' page, TED and Dropbox.

part 2

Tactical MBA thinking: how to organise resources

Tactic, n. ['*takt* ɪ *k*] a method used or a course of action followed in order to achieve an immediate or short-term aim

The conventional view of tactics is that they are what you use to deliver strategy. Tactical thinking includes the day-to-day implementation of agreed goals and describes the kind of decision making that adjusts to the problems, dilemmas and choices every manager meets as they do their job. What you do in those moments to keep your head above water is tactical and this thinking occupies the majority of a middle manager's day. It involves:

▌ organising the resources in a business to create value (remember, this is every manager's aim)

▌ using multiple methods for observation and measurement and repeated cycles of trial and error

▌ making incremental improvements (not reinventing the wheel)

▌ communication

▌ short- to medium-term planning and making relatively reversible decisions.

Tactical thinking uses a sequential or **lineal** approach. If tactics are not aligned to the strategy of the organisation, then the strategy can quickly come unstuck and, when this happens, lower levels of management can find themselves trapped in office or corporate politics. There are three types of resource essential to creating value in a company:

1. processes and operations, and how they are planned and improved

2. people, and what they do

3. money, and the microeconomics behind financial decisions.

Tactical thinking is a bit like navigating towards a destination on a sailing ship. You are clear about where you are heading, but your course is affected by changing winds and by the movements of currents in the sea around you. You keep on course by constantly adjusting sails to get the most out of the conditions. The people, the processes and the cash in your business are a bit like the sails on a ship. In this part, we will see in turn how each of these resources is organised as a function.

Processes and operations
Where design, decision and function meet

'Begin at the beginning,' the King said, very gravely,
'and go on till you come to the end: then stop.'

Lewis Carroll, *Alice in Wonderland*

In a nutshell

All managers are day-to-day operations managers. Whether
in the private or public sector, in for-profit or not-for-profit,
large or small organisations, at the top or the bottom, almost
every aspect of management can be seen as a contribution
to activities that are organised, planned and subject to
evaluation. In short, they manage processes that make up the
operations that deliver the goods and services.

In this chapter you will:

▌ learn about the background, context and scope of the
operations function

▌ define the difference between tactical and strategic
management of operations

▌ apply the input–transformation–output model to processes

▌ explore supply chain management

'Doing' is a process

Processes are activities that transform inputs to outputs. An operation may consist of many processes. For an MBA, it is essential to know something about processes and operations because:

▌ no other subject gets this close to analysing what an organisation does; doing what you do well may be the only difference between you and your competitors

▌ equally, the operations function has a strong claim for being where future strategy is translated into present activity; all strategy must, at some point, be turned into a process that works.

This is a function always with one eye on today and another on tomorrow.

DAY BY DAY PRACTICE

1 Contact someone in your network and arrange to visit some of the operations of their organisation. Be curious and ask questions while you are there and, later, write a reflective account of what you saw. Compare with the processes you know. What was different? What was similar? What made you stop and think?

2 Identify a known issue facing your business about which you can make a prediction. How will that issue affect how the business operates?

These questions illustrate the all-pervasive nature of operations and process management and the tension between how things are best organised now versus what needs to be planned to prepare for the future. These twin tasks form the context for the management of processes and operations.

Designing an Initial Response Service (IRS)

British government policy aims at parity between mental and physical health provision, and one obstacle for patients, carers and mental health professionals has been how difficult it is to get a response after a call for help. For mental health trusts, managing appropriate levels of support quickly and efficiently not only saves on resources and time, it reduces distress.

The leadership team at Northumberland, Tyne and Wear NHS Foundation Trust (NTW), based in Sunderland, took on this challenge. Despite a hard-working and dedicated staff, delays caused by crisis teams being tied up in other cases were tying up scarce and more expensive stop-gaps from other public services, such as the police. With no central coordinating system in place, referrals often were bounced around from one part of the system to another.

NTW gathered a team of people, including experts in operations transformation who had worked at the local Nissan car factory. Their vast experience of operations management was brought to bear on analysis of every part of the patient pathway, which is the journey from referral (or call for help) to discharge.

The Initial Response Service (IRS) was the result. All referrals and external calls are now routed to a single point with one telephone number. Non-clinical staff are robustly trained to take calls, triage and manage requests for information, advice, help and support from clinical staff as required. The service is available 24/7 and is open to everyone. Having multidisciplinary teams based in one place means response can be appropriate to crisis, up to and including going to see someone face-to-face in the community within an hour.

Since going live:

- admission of Sunderland residents to psychiatric intensive care wards has halved and is below the national benchmark, while the proportion of those admitted who were detained under the Mental Health Act increased (this suggests much better diagnosis)

- a new street triage service has been set up, with trained police officers embedded in the IRS, and there has been a tenfold reduction in the number of people being detained (sectioned) for psychiatric assessment

- GPs have direct and round-the-clock contact with every level of service and advice in one call, cutting back on paperwork and time access

- over 50 per cent of referrals now come direct from those who use the service, including carers and families, as well as older people and those with learning disabilities. More than 80 per cent of calls are non-clinical, with individuals asking for advice and information about services or appointments

- only 1 per cent of all calls result in crisis home treatment and less than 0.5 per cent in admission. Median length of stay for those who use services has fallen from 23 to 15 days compared to a national benchmark of 32 days

- finally, psychiatric bed costs have fallen by £3.5 million per year.

Adapted from 'Valued care in mental health: Improving for excellence' (2018), NHS Improvement.[1]

The context of managing processes and operations

It is useful to take the process view to understand a business because the effective and efficient management of operations is what generates value for the organisation. Tactical decision making in operations management is aimed at maintaining the capacity to meet the current needs and satisfy customers and stakeholders. To achieve this, operations management tends to break things down to constituent parts. Accordingly, operations management is about the design, implementation, evaluation and improvement of the systems that deliver goods, products or services of a business in the here and now. First-level managers typically focus on small-scale processes or single steps in bigger operations and may find themselves working purely at this level in their functional area. Strategic decision making, at the other end, looks at providing goals for the future needs and senior managers have to see how the types of process make sense in the context of the organisation as a whole. The responsibility for bridging this capacity gap sits with middle managers.

As a middle manager, you may be given responsibility for groups of steps or entire complex processes. Operations management will involve the design, implementation, evaluation and improvement of processes that bridge the gap between the present and the future. Managers at this level have the sometimes difficult task of doing two things at once – aligning to strategic plans and requirements set from above while making sure the current set up runs smoothly. Although the tactical and strategic levels (the short term and longer term) should work in harmony, in reality this is far from easy. There are several reasons for this:

▌ **Language and culture:** different organisations – and parts inside an organisation – define processes and their boundaries in different ways. Finding a common language, dealing with politics and navigating the unwritten rules of how an organisation functions all require time and effort. After mergers, acquisitions or international expansions, this can be a significant factor.

▌ **Complexity:** the more processes are grouped together, the higher the level of complexity.

▌ **Uncertainty:** the more an organisation projects into the future, the less it can be certain about where, when and how value will be generated.

When managing processes, some prefer what British researcher Peter Checkland called a 'hard systems' approach, which uses an engineering mindset and simplifies the model of the system to lineal cause and effect.[2] Here, many people just enjoy 'getting on with the job' in a nuts and bolts sort of way. By contrast, a 'soft systems' approach sees problems as ill-defined and process in terms of the varied views of all concerned. In practice, both approaches constitute the various models in use today.

Input, transformation, output (ITO): process mapping

There are three basic organising concepts needed for any process:

Inputs: which are either resources being transformed or resources being used to transform. For example, in a winery, the grapes used to make a wine are the resources that are being transformed. In contrast, the knowledge required to judge the right time to harvest the grapes, the people who work in the winery, the vats, barrels and bottles in which the wine matures, and the money borrowed from the bank are all inputs used to transform something else. Inputs can be physical or abstract and may come from elements outside the organisation such as suppliers.

Transformation: or the part of the process where value is added by, for example, a material transformation or a change in physical location, ownership, or purpose and use. In the winery, this might involve not just the time it takes for the wine to ferment but also the management of the expectations of customers (perhaps in terms of branding).

Outputs: goods and services, as well as any waste or by-products from the transformation step. Outputs may be for external or internal customers, or other processes. Outputs, in the winery, would include the wine in labelled bottles, and also the residues from cleaning the equipment or the skins from the grapes.

Highly structured processes in assembly-line manufacturing, such as the automotive industry, have provided much of the background and terminology used in operations management. But, even if you're managing in a company whose products are intangible services, what you do can be understood in terms of inputs, transformations and outputs.

Process maps, rich pictures and decision-trees

When you need to get detail, a visual way of mapping the passage of any good or service is by using process flow charts. These can be a useful starting point for defining, describing and analysing exactly how your business works. Process flow charts can be made at three levels:

1. **High-level:** covers the major events in the process only.
2. **Detailed:** has every step mapped, including decision points, queues and feedback loops.
3. **Swim-lane:** extends to show detail of actions by the multiple roles in the process.

Process flow charts are OK for constructing the *flow* of an operation at a very broad level but can quickly become bogged down in technical detail if you try to map everything that happens or could happen. They are also limited in identifying issues that are not part of a process. For that, rich pictures, developed by systems thinker Peter Checkland, are a fantastic way to gather information about a complex situation (see Figure 3.1, for example). Using drawings or pictures to think about issues frees your mind to create links and associations and to see patterns. Rich pictures can uncover not just how processes work but also how people see them. Symbols are used, but much more freely. There are few rules in how to create one, but the instructions in the activity below may guide you.

FIGURE 3.1 A rich picture

A rich picture needn't have too many components to be effective or insightful. This simple but powerful image was a prompt for a long discussion on career direction and personal development.

Another method useful to pinpointing process issues of cause and effect is an Ishikawa or fishbone diagram (see Figure 3.2), named after its inventor and resemblance, respectively. Place the effect of an issue on the right-hand side and draw a horizontal line to the left. Branching out from this, above and below, come a number of diagonal lines, each representing a category of cause and, on each of these, horizontal lines can be used to generate possible causes. Categories of causes in manufacturing, product or service industries will differ. Typically, a manufacturing root cause exercise would look at categories such as methods, machines, materials, or people and measurement. For products or services, such as in the example on the following page, categories such as promotion, place, people and process would be better, but there are no hard and fast rules. Choose whatever generates most ideas and creativity.

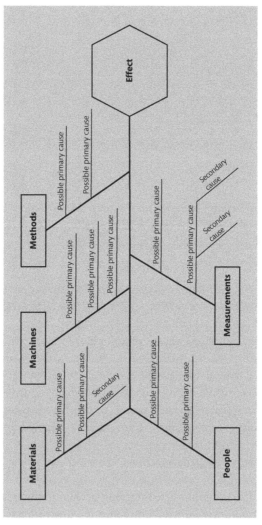

FIGURE 3.2 An Ishikawa or fishbone cause and effect diagram

DAY BY DAY PRACTICE

1 Create a rich picture of your role at work. Colours, images and metaphors are encouraged. Have fun drawing it, but make sure the elements are connected. Use words only when a picture won't work.

(a) Start with structure (the parts of the situation that are stable).

(b) Then look for what moves in the process (e.g. activities).

(c) Pay attention to how they interact with each other but try not to get stuck in the theoretical functional silos. Rich pictures should show how things actually are.

(d) Don't forget feelings, emotions and behaviour. Include yourself in the picture.

2 Identify an issue or problem in your working situation and identify it by its effect. Then work to create your own fishbone diagram to surface some of the root causes. Working with others increases the potential to spot something new.

Types of processes

Manufacturing operations can be broken down into five process types to reflect how much flexibility is needed in either the process or the product. These are as follows:

▌ **Ad hoc project:** one-off, customised or occasional projects. These can take a long time to complete and may themselves contain the other process types. Coordinated response to a natural disaster, such as a hurricane or earthquake, is an ad hoc project, for example.

▌ **Job shop:** high variety but low volume, jobbing processes are ready to provide a wide range of products or services with little repetition. Specialist precision toolmakers, London's bespoke tailors in Savile Row and online greetings card provider Moonpig.com are examples.

Then there are three sorts of flow:

▌ **Batch:** longer runs with less variety than job lots. Outputs are similar but may be large or small in number (a village baker produces small batches of bread; modern agricultural methods can produce very large batches of chickens).

▌ **Line:** high-volume manufacture or assembly of standardised components. The automotive assembly process is a familiar example, as would be the majority of garment production in much of the world.

▌ **Continuous:** largely automated, very high volume with relatively high costs associated in set up and cessation. A Pepsi bottling plant, for example, will run at high speed and continuously for high volumes of a small variety of products.

The operations function in any organisation may be geared to achieving one of two things:

1 **Agility,** that is, the ability for the whole organisation to respond with speed to major changes in the environment or in demand.

2 **Lean,** which is the goal of an operations process that has eliminated all waste in input, transformation or output.

Service-sector processes and operations fall into three types of process:

▌ **Professional:** high variety, low volume, where a long time may be spent in contact between provider and customer. Lawyers, doctors and bespoke technical support or consulting are examples.

▌ **Service 'shop':** most of our service interactions involve some customisation, but are, essentially, held within limits of variety. Buying something in a shop, renting a car or staying in a hotel are all services that fit into this category.

▌ **Mass:** many customer transactions with almost no customisation. The provider of the service needs little judgement to do their job and the customer may be going through a routine. In mature economies, many of these services are now automated (for example, self-service supermarket checkouts, airport self-service check-ins).

Supply chain management

Supply chain management is oversight (i.e. planning and control) of the relationships between the various activities of the 'journey' of goods and services to customers. It may involve elements such as procurement that are outside the direct control of the organisation. The overall idea is that the manager needs to ensure that all this ends up with some value added, usually expressed in terms of margin or profit. It is not always such a simple task, however, partly because the meaning behind the concept of value is, as we have seen, in the eye of the beholder.

A supply chain network consists of all the components that are needed to source, transform and deliver what an organisation makes or does to its customers. It includes not just the physical locations and proprietary logistical or support systems but also the contracts and agreements with first- and second-tier suppliers of raw materials, outsourced functions that are part of value creation, and methods of evaluation of customer satisfaction. All these aspects need decision making that remains alert to the strategic goals of the organisation, the behaviours of competitors and stakeholders, economies of scale, and impacts on fixed costs and investment.

The idea that operations cross the boundaries of all primary, support and managerial activities was captured by Michael Porter in the supply chain model in the 1980s. Porter envisaged two types of activity in a firm – primary and support. Primary activities run in sequenced silos from supply and inbound logistics, through whatever operations the organisation performs to transform inputs to outputs, delivery of those outputs in distribution, followed by marketing and sales and leading to after sales service and support. There is some debate as to how idealised this sequence is, as many organisations don't fit the traditional assembly-line analogy, but it does focus on differentiation what is directly value creating (i.e. what contributes directly to what the customer pay for) and what is indirectly enabling those elements. These are processes that weave into all the primary activities, and are the infrastructure (departments that manage resources), human resource management, technology, and procurement. Again, the problem with the Value Chain has been its bluntness in adapting to real world organisations which have different business models or requirements. Taken as prescriptive, it can make things look a bit "cookie-cutter". Taken as descriptive, its outlines are rather too broad and rigid in fluid business contexts, and it completely ignores the culture or mission of the organisation.

Nevertheless, today this remains an influential, integrating model. Porter expected this tool to be used in decision making specifically to exploit competitive advantage, but it is often used now for justifying the structures and relationships between primary and support functions in organisations.

Measuring supply chain success

One widely used framework you may find useful for evaluating process management is the Supply Chain Operations Reference (SCOR), developed by the APICS Supply Chain Council (APICS SCC).[3] It summarises the language and definitions used in the design of the supply chain and allows users to model a process, benchmark performance against KPIs (key performance indicators), as well as learn from others' **best practice**. There are five basic types of process in SCOR, each one a relationship between a supplier and a customer:

1. **Source:** all procurement and delivery, including from your supplier's supplier to your supplier.

2. **Make:** adding value in production through transformation of goods and services.

3. **Deliver:** to the customer of the goods or services.

4. **Plan:** preparation, oversight and management of all links in the chain.

5. **Return:** handling reverse flow, usually from complaint or default after delivery.

How to measure process: flow, inventory and capacity

Sensible process measurements are important for planning, control and improvement. Let's consider the fundamentals:

- **Flow** is measured in the throughput time, or how long it would take to perform a given process on a product or service with no delays or waiting along the way.

- **Capacity** is the throughput rate, measured as how many or how much of something can be processed within the resources allocated for it.

Whatever is sitting around in between transformative processes on its way to the customer is referred to as inventory or work in progress.

Lead times, or the delays between initiating and completing an order, can be deliberately longer than process times, and sometimes much longer than they should be. The delivery time refers to how long something actually takes and this may be much longer than the process time (flow). Generally, the shorter you can make the delivery time, the more efficient,

or leaner, your process will be and the greater the amount
of feedback from more iterations of the process you will get.
Because of the delicate relationship between supply, demand
and price, any change in capacity – which can lead or lag
demand – requires careful consideration and planning. One
way of smoothing the ups and downs in supply–demand
capacity changes is through inventory management. Here,
though, there are other risks, such as what your competitors
are doing and what additional capital costs might be incurred.

Little's Law, a mathematical relationship, is often used to
show the relationship between these three elements of an
operation:

$$throughput\ time\ (flow) = work\ in\ progress\ (inventory)/$$
$$throughput\ rate\ (capacity)$$

Different businesses will denote different types of units in
flow management (e.g. producers, customers, cash, etc.),
but the principle has proved very adaptable for many stable
processes. For example, at an airport check-in, from the
passenger's perspective, value is a function of (i) how long
it takes to walk up to a counter and for the official to make a
decision (throughput time), (ii) how many desks are manned
(capacity) and (iii) how many people are in the queue doing
nothing (work in progress). However, other stakeholders,
working from exactly the same data, may derive a completely
different evaluation of value added.

Planning, control and feedback

Every operation requires some form of measurement.
Operational measurement can be part of a planning process
to encourage radical progress in a new direction. In terms
of control, it could be used to identify where there are gaps
between current performance and targets or benchmarks, or
simply to confirm where things stand at a given moment.
In such cases, managers often look to identify bottlenecks.

In response to the lean movement, the Theory of Constraints (TOC) was developed by Eliyahu Goldratt to show the business case for how every effort should be made to manage to the narrowest point in a system, as opposed to the idea of managing quality at every stage (see below).[4]

Quality: measurement, evaluation and improvement

Quality control probably has ancient roots in buyers checking what suppliers were selling them before taking possession (rather like opening the box of eggs at the supermarket before you pay). As manufacturing technology grew in sophistication, methodical sampling tools such as statistical process control (SPC) were developed to identify defects during production that could pre-empt an end user's refusal. This quality control phase moved on to the idea of quality assurance and eventually to quality management, which pervades every step and stage of every process in an operation – with the goal of making sampling redundant and the idea of an unhappy customer an impossibility.

One person closely associated with this was the US academic W. Edward Deming, famous for his 'plan-do-check-act' cycle of continuous improvement. Deming inspired the development of high value-added manufacturing in Japan in the 1960s and 1970s. He was famously quoted as saying that 94 per cent of problems in quality are systemic and the responsibility of management, rather than simple instances of error.[5]

A systemic embrace of a 'people' aspect in improving output is core to the concept of total quality management that took hold in the 1980s, even in sectors where the emphasis had been only on the reduction of defective units in production lines. TQM was widely adopted and promoted as a way of cutting cost and waste. It has since been built on as a holistic, organisation-wide effort to reach the same levels of attention to detail attained in manufacturing in every function of a business. Perhaps the most famous example of TQM in action is the 'just-in-time' philosophy of continuous improvement or kaizen the Toyota Production System (TPS), which was a precursor to the lean manufacturing movement.

DAY BY DAY PRACTICE

1 How is quality measured in your work?

2 Revisit your answer to the question at the start of this chapter about a known issue in the future. What do you know that will have an impact on your organisation's readiness? How would you go about communicating this to senior management?

Putting it together: value creation is a process, too

Processes and the operations they comprise are basic to the concept of value creation. Every firm will have developed, over time, its own set of procedures. Managing groups of processes in an operation well is a very important aspect of what managers do. Managing those who manage operations represents the coordinated efforts of an organisation to employ models of excellence and these can have a real impact. It is impossible to do any of this without a sufficient level of technical competency.

It is worth noting that we have adopted a machine metaphor to explain these processes and how they fit together. The real test of this way of thinking is the interface with people. This is notoriously difficult to get right. Improvement initiatives such as business process re-engineering (BPR) have proved unsustainable as times and fashions have changed around them, though successors such as the ISO 9000 series or Motorola's Six Sigma continue to rely on the same *paradigm*.

QUESTIONS FOR REFLECTION

1 Draw a mind map or a rich picture of a personal system that you are part of. This could be your family, a social group you are a member of, or your community. Make a few notes on anything that occurs to you, and remember that explaining your picture to another person can reveal a lot.

2 What would you be doing in life if you knew that money would not be a problem?

Further reading

A classic text:	*Images of Organization*, by Gareth Morgan (1997), 2nd edition, Sage.
Going deeper:	*Operations Management,* 8th edition, by Nigel Slack (2016), FT Prentice Hall. A comprehensive overview of the whole topic, with a lot of supplementary material online.
Watch these:	A hotel operations manager is interviewed about his job and career. Filmed in 2011, but with a number of lessons relevant for anyone involved in operations management: **https://icould. com/stories/bruce-r/**.
	'How whisky is made', a short video published by VisitScotland introducing this important process (at least in my view!): **https://www.youtube.com/ watch?v=ZNe4ZRFx9oY**.

Notes

1 https://improvement.nhs.uk/resources/valued-care-mental-health-improving-excellence/.

2 Checkland, P. and Scholes, J. (2009) *Soft Systems Methodology: A 30-year Retrospection*, John Wiley & Sons.

3 http://www.apics.org/apics-for-business/frameworks/scor, accessed April 2019.

4 Goldratt, E. (1990) *Theory of Constraints*, North River Press.

5 Deming, W.E. (2013) in Orsini, J. (ed.) *The Essential Deming: Leadership Principles from the Father of Quality*, McGraw-Hill Professional.

People
4

Humans are renewable energy for business

Hell is other people.

Jean-Paul Sartre

In a nutshell

Businesses are run by people. Great businesses are run by talented people, at all levels. The challenging job of managing this human resource mix belongs to all managers, not only HR professionals or the CEO. Just as with the operations function, your job is to ensure efficient implementation of what is needed right now while, at the same time, preparing and planning to be able to deliver the future strategy.

Although there is consensus that people are vital to the success of a business, there is no agreement as to what that means. This chapter will provide background and structure to what is often a complex topic.

In this chapter you will:

▌ trace the historical development of managing people

▌ examine the external and internal contexts of the HR function

▌ study corporate culture and the evolution of the employment relationship

▌ investigate the role played by people in managing quality

Managing people in a modern organisation

Organisations have always relied on finding, developing and keeping the right staff to carry out all the functions of the enterprise, but what this means in practice has changed in the different eras of management.

▌ **Nineteenth to mid-twentieth century:** the age of the personnel department, where people are a resource that can be quantified and costed, their output measured and their recruitment prepared for. This view has its roots in the rapid expansion of workforce need during early and middle stages of the industrial revolution in Europe. Partly in reaction to this new economic model, this revolution was also the age of social reform and the unionisation of labour in many parts of the world.

▌ **From mid-twentieth century:** the age of organisational behaviour (OB) and human resource management (HRM), where people are an essential expression of the culture of the organisation. The entry into the workforce of many more women during the Second World War helped change definitions of labour, and heralded an age in which the development of the transnational or multinational company, sophisticated performance management systems, mass production and, more recently, the shift from manufacturing to service and knowledge-based economies have all played a part. Later, there was mass privatisation and a reduction in unionisation, as well as a movement towards collaboration and empowerment for individuals at work.

▌ **Twenty-first century:** in developed economies, a new age of partnering with stakeholders, fuelled by globalisation and enabled by technology. People are seen as the source of creativity and innovation. Long gone are the days of the monolithic corporate personnel function; HR is now decentralised, and knowledge capital and inter-connectedness are the priorities. In emerging economies, population demographics have begun to exert a drive of their own.

It is the line manager's job to get things done. This is impossible without people, but that presents unique challenges because this is a topic soaked in theories and counter-theories from psychology and sociology. At first, 'people' seems like a topic that lacks the crisp, neat edges MBAs are often so fond of. But, all other things being equal, organisations can be differentiated only by their talent. For this reason, HR has a vital link to strategy.

DAY BY DAY PRACTICE

Identify the head of human resources in your organisation. Arrange to interview them if you can.

1 How has their job changed in the last five years?

2 What factors will influence how the organisation manages people in the next five years?

When you have done this, reflect on your own experience managing or being managed by others.

Over the last 25 years, line managers have taken direct control of traditional HR functions such as scoping job requirements, running recruitment, performance review and reward, employee motivation and promoting organisational culture. HR professionals are now more likely to act as specialists or consultants to be called on when needed. It is middle management – already under pressure to take on work and respond to every interruption and stimulus – that has added managing people to an already long list of responsibilities. The result is a core area of management where everyone has first-hand experience (and opinions) but rarely any formal training.

The external context: macro-culture

National culture is often the topic of description and opinion, but rarely of insight. Many organisations now recruit and work across many borders so the need to manage an international, diverse resource has also grown. Perhaps the most famous attempt to study the interplay between regional/national cultural preferences and corporate culture (initially, that of IBM) is by Geert Hofstede.[1] Given the free flow of human resources around the world and the global nature of management as a career, you might think about how these apply (or will apply) to your own experience.

There are six dimensions of values in his theory:

▌ **Power distance:** how a society handles inequality in the distribution of power and resources. Large power distance accepts hierarchies in which everyone has and knows their place. In low power distance countries, people look for equality and minimisation of power.

▌ **Individualism vs collectivism:** which takes prominence, the 'I', or the 'we'? Individualism is a preference for looking after your immediate circle. Collectivism stands for a tighter expectation of loyalties to an extended family or wider social networks.

▌ **Masculinity vs femininity:** masculinity as a dimension represents a societal bias for success through competition, achievement and material rewards. The other aspect, femininity, values success as cooperation and consensus and an aim for quality of life.

▌ **Uncertainty avoidance:** the extent to which you and those in your society feel uncomfortable with the unknown or with

ambiguity. Hofstede sees this as being an orientation to the
uncertainties of the future – resulting in either strong codes
of behaviour that do not tolerate dissent (high), or social
norms that are more open to 'bending the rules' (weak).

Pragmatic vs normative: a pragmatic society is one where
people accept that there is a lot of complexity in life which
may be impossible to explain fully. The purpose of life is
to live it, and truth is contextual, material things transient.
Under a normative orientation, there is a wish to find in
explanation the objective 'truth'. Traditions and the past are
treasured, spending is encouraged and adaptability is valued.

Indulgence vs restraint: the sixth, and most recent,
dimension contrasts indulgence, in which a society
pursues happiness freely as a basic human motive of
having fun, with restraint, in which such an urge is
regulated or suppressed by social norms.

The interesting thing about culture is that we only really know
ours by contrasting it with another. On a small scale this is
obvious – we frequently see differences among the people,
families and organisations around us. We take a lot of things for
granted and correctly locating our perceptions of the world,
especially if we are managers, is much more difficult. Sensitivity
to cultural values and norms is important, but as a manager
you need to be aware of what is happening in a wider context.
Consider how each of the following affects you in your workplace:

The political and legal environment: in the European
Union (EU), for example, member countries have agreed
to subordinate some national legislative decision making
and this has had an effect on employment laws and the
free flow of people to work. The legal framework governing
ethical behaviour is also important.

Demographics: the global population will continue to grow
over the next 60–70 years. Despite a falling fertility rate
globally, some countries will struggle to meet the demands of

their ageing populations, while others will have to contend
with rapidly expanding populations moving into ever-larger
urban areas. Chapter 12 will look at this in more detail.

▍ **Education:** policies that prepare future generations for
work require educational systems that align.

▍ **Globalisation and international careers:** the proven
ability to work well across borders and cultures, and in
increasingly diverse teams, will be one of the tests for
talent management in the future.

DAY BY DAY PRACTICE

1 How were you recruited to your current position?
Did your organisation take into account any of the
macro-level factors above? If you can, go and check
your reasoning with your head of HR or line manager.

2 Think about your national culture. Where do you think
it sits on each of Hofstede's measures of culture? Now
think about the culture of a current or past organisation
you know. Is it the same or different?

We've looked at those things outside the organisation, the ones
that set the parameters for how an organisation behaves, and
now we will look at the manager's tasks at the organisational
level – that is, those things that affect your daily job.

The internal context: organisations and micro-cultures

Details and circumstances may vary from company to
company but, when it comes to employing people, there are
really only two constants that make a difference:

1 A contract of employment between the organisation and
the person.

2 The contribution of the contract to our sense of identity, achievement and purpose.

We might spend more than a third of our lives at our places of work so it is no surprise that we feel an attachment that cannot be explained merely by being paid. For many, the idea of culture as a shared set of behaviours feels like common sense.

What is culture? Some describe it as 'the way we do things round here'. The veteran US organisation expert Edgar Schein sees organisational culture as operating below the surface, but evident at three levels:[2]

▌**Level 1 – artefacts:** the physical locations, interiors, uniforms (formal or informal) or outward signs of branding.

▌**Level 2 – espoused values:** the norms and shared beliefs carried by the employees (articulated occasionally in a mission statement, but often more evident from procedures and rules).

▌**Level 3 – basic assumptions:** the sub-conscious of the 'corporate person', deeply held values, the ultimate test being how much tolerance there is for diverse types of behaviours or decision making.

US MBAs place people management under the umbrella of 'organisational behaviour' (OB). It sounds as though an organisation can 'behave' just as an individual person can. This could reflect a pattern in the employment contract between a firm and an individual that is part of the national culture in the USA, but actually the idea of OB travels quite well. The organisational design template for many multinational companies follows a similar set of beliefs about hard work, independence and the rights of the individual. It's not hard to see why many managers regard good management of their human resource as a source of competitive advantage (see Chapter 7). However, HR practice is often less than sophisticated. When a human resource issue is mishandled, an otherwise competent manager can find themselves in hot water very quickly and talented staff can be left demotivated, disillusioned and looking elsewhere.

In fact, studies of what managers actually do at work are a fairly recent phenomenon. It was Henry Mintzberg who pointed out that managers don't spend their time in secluded luxury issuing commands. He observed them being put under pressure, being interrupted and dealing with things as they came up. He was able, though, to identify three main management roles:[3]

1 **Informational:** internally, sometimes as official spokesperson and sometimes informally, act as mentor and the driver to disseminate communication in the organisation, as well as be the channel for information to the external environment as liaison.

2 **Decisional:** get things moving and implement change projects, adjudicate disputes and handle conflicts or unexpected situations decisively, allocate resources and negotiate with external stakeholders.

3 **Interpersonal:** be a symbolic figurehead or motivational leader and build a connecting network of information sources external to your organisation.

Managing people means managing the one resource that is everywhere in your organisation. Your ability to analyse the multiple and complex factors influencing this organisational balance is terribly important and it certainly helps to have on hand some tools and techniques to help you cope with this. A robust diagnostic first step for this is to use the McKinsey 7-S framework, a matrix very often applied by MBAs. It was born in an era of consultancy and reinvention of management structures in the United States in the

1980s, in a period of internationalisation, globalisation and shift from manufacturing and production to knowledge and information management. The seven elements in the framework were therefore an attempt to redress a balance skewed toward quantitative analysis and measurement in strategic thinking and include what are often called (somewhat anachronistically, given how difficult they can be to master) a set of soft skills or ideas, such as style and staff.

At heart, 7-S is intended for use in identifying competitive advantage, which is one view of strategy among several (see Chapter 7), and there is no doubting its flexibility and universal appeal. At its heart is the S of Shared Values, which is interesting to note because it surfaces the simple, guiding ideas around which the organisation is built. As we shall see when we look at Strategy later, this should be simple and abstract enough to generate meaning inside the organisation, even if outsiders may not understand them.

The matrix consists of:

Strategy: the overall objectives and the requirements to meet them.

Structure: the hierarchy, organisation of tasks or functions and divisions of labour.

Systems: the processes and operations used to get things done, e.g. the supply chain.

Shared values: the original intention of the organisation, its founding purpose and resulting core beliefs.

Style: more or less equivalent to Schein's level 2 of culture, the unwritten rules.

Staff: the potential represented by the collective of people in the organisation.

Skills: what the organisation (not the individuals in it) is good at.

The 7-S framework is a little harder to apply than it looks because it supposes all the information you need is easily accessible, and clearly some of these factors are intangible. You will also need honesty in admitting where there are internal contradictions in your organisation.

DAY BY DAY PRACTICE

Conduct an analysis of your organisation using the 7-S framework:

1 In the short term: do any of the seven aspects of culture feel like 'hot spots' in your organisation? Which one would you work on first? Put this analysis on one side for a while.

2 In the long term: over time (MBAs always want to do things too quickly; it would be better if they slowed down), develop your understanding of these seven ways of looking at your organisation. You might, for example, revisit your first analysis every six months to see what has changed.

Using McKinsey's 7-S as its framework, Tom Peters and Robert Waterman's 1984 book *In Search of Excellence* was, for a while, seen as having all the answers when it came to company culture and corporate success.[4] Unfortunately, many of the companies showcased failed in the years that followed, and the lure of culture and 'excellence' as predictors of success faded. The lesson from this is that to understand culture you must link it to performance and value creation (and usually this means the bottom line). The fundamental question remains: how do you, as a manager, best represent the interests of the founders and owners?

When it comes to managing people, value can be quantified in terms of productivity. The classic ingredients for this are measurement of what people know and what they can do.

Measuring productivity in people management

As we've seen, in the old days HR was about job analysis
and the processes needed for selection of personnel with the
right qualifications. This is still needed, but what is different
is these activities now have to align talent to strategy. The
individual desires and wants of employees are not the driver,
though shaping the organisational culture means managing
a delicate balance between all stakeholders and making
everyone feel valued and informed. HR professionals work to
exert this cultural influence with three tools:

- **Recruitment and retention:** selecting for cultural fit,
  because 'not fitting in' is arguably a more common reason
  for leaving a job than a lack of talent or dissatisfaction
  with pay.

- **Training and development:** from induction onwards,
  training and internal communication need to enable
  people to understand the cultural norms and engage
  emotionally.

- **Motivation and rewards:** the balance of give and take in an
  organisation, of which money is only one aspect, is crucial
  in communicating values and purpose.

These things matter to you, too. A manager is there to get
things done and as soon as the work to be done exceeds the
resource available to do it, workforce planning becomes a
part of every general manager's role. To undertake this, you
need to gain a basic understanding (at least) of:

- organisational design and structure (luckily, you're in one,
  so you can at least study that)

- job design, recruitment, selection and role development
  (using the HR professionals to assist and guide, plus your
  own reflections)

- talent retention and management.

Performance and reward

HR specialists are probably still the ones, even in smaller organisations, who take first responsibility for recommending financial rewards and they may also oversee the development and deployment of policies to evaluate employee performance. But what these practices and policies look like will vary, depending on national location and culture, company history and strategic intent. Without doubt, the organisation will also want you to pay most attention to performance. When you are in tune with the policies of your organisation, all this can be a very smooth ride. When you're not, it will dramatically interfere with your job, though you will have no one else to blame but yourself if that happens. I'll consider management involvement in performance from three perspectives – motivation, teamwork and the individual's performance.

Motivation: job satisfaction and happiness at work

US psychologist Frederick Herzberg's two-factor theory of motivation and satisfaction prompted a change in how we understand people's engagement with their jobs.[5] Herzberg agreed with the idea that human beings have a set of needs and desires and that achieving these is what motivates us. Abraham Maslow had earlier presented a hierarchy of needs, arranged in a pyramid with basic physiological requirements such as shelter at the base and self-actualisation (never fully defined) at the summit.[6] Herzberg thought, however, that motivation was a bit more complex. Basic needs demotivate us when they are absent but do not add to our happiness when present. Higher-level needs provide real satisfaction and these are what we truly seek. Herzberg saw two independently functioning factors:

▎ **Motivators:** these include being challenged by our work, receiving recognition, achievement or personal growth.

When present in our workplace, they give us meaning. They are also all concerned with carrying out tasks. When absent, they tend to make us feel less worthwhile and less competent, which is deeply dissatisfying.

- **Hygiene factors:** these are necessary because, when present, they prevent demotivation. However, they do not intrinsically lead to motivation when they are present. Examples include salary, fringe benefits and bonuses, and these will form the context of carrying out tasks, but not what brings us real satisfaction.

If this sounds like common sense, it may be that it is. But, like many basic business concepts, 'the devil is in the detail' and the infinite variation that arises in each particular situation (remember Schön and his swampy lowlands) produces dilemmas for you as a manager. For example, how important do you think praise for a job well done is in motivating a team? In some people and teams it won't be valued, while for others it may be more significant than pay. Maslow and Herzberg's are theories that point to motivation towards desirable goals or ends. Other theories focus on means, or the processes of motivation. Vroom's expectancy theory says that people will choose a way of acting depending on their expectation of the result (the end dictates the means), so managers must remember that motivation is the relationship between effort and result in people's minds.

It's not a big jump from this to the idea known as the psychological contract (see Figure 4.1), which is a way of measuring how employer and employee see their mutual obligations in employment. At one end of the spectrum, it is as a *social exchange*, where psychological well-being, belonging and loyalty are highly valued. At the other end, it is as an *economic exchange*, a transaction of time for money with no expectation of an emotional or long-term attachment.

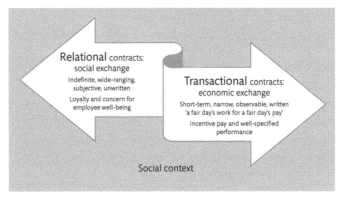

FIGURE 4.1 The psychological contract
Source: Adapted from Rousseau, D.M. (1995) *Psychological Contracts in Organizations: Understanding Written and Unwritten Agreements*, Sage Publications, Inc. Reproduced with permission.

The nature of work, however, is undergoing change at a rate unprecedented since the very first days of the industrial revolution. We're now used to flat and matrix management structures, the movement of services and jobs around the world, and the pressures on equality and diversity in the workplace, but these are trends from the past acting on the present. We are now more in tune with the 'human' in human resource management than we used to be.

CASE STUDY

Breaking the Silence

David Beeney enjoyed a successful career in media and achieved his goal of becoming the managing director of a regional daily newspaper by the age of only 35. His career continued to blossom and he rose to become one of the commercial directors of Auto Trader. Despite David's success, he hid a huge secret from everybody in his life, both professionally and personally, until 16 May 2016 when he outed himself about his mental health. The decision to open up and be honest about his life-long struggles with panic attacks and anxiety has changed his life dramatically.

David founded Breaking the Silence Ltd[7] in October 2016 and in only two years he has become one of the leading advisers in the UK on how you create cultures in the workplace that are free from the stigma of mental ill-health. He demonstrates the link between well-being strategy and business results and how the creation of kinder environments drives employee energy levels. His clients include HSBC, Virgin Media, TUI, Direct Line, Sainsbury's and the NHS and, in 2018, he was named one of the top 101 influencers globally on employee engagement.

David struggles to understand why so many boardrooms still regard mental health awareness as a fluffy subject, focusing on numbers more than the well-being of their people. Senior leaders need to set the tone from the top of their organisation by sharing how mental health has touched their own lives. He believes that too many CEOs lose their job because they are scared to share vulnerability, seeing it as a weakness. He coaches senior leaders to understand that when you share vulnerability, you inspire those around you and strengthen your position as the head of an organisation.

Managers tend not to speak to staff about mental health because they do not feel qualified. The great news is that they do not need to be. When Breaking the Silence delivers mental health workshops, it trains managers on the benefits of kindness rather than increasing knowledge of mental health. To quote David, 'It took me five years to qualify as a mental health counsellor and it's still a tough job. You can't send managers on a two-day course and expect them to come back qualified to fix people.' David believes that the job of a people manager with regard to mental health is twofold. ▶

> First comes creating a personable relationship where employees feel safe to open up. Then it's a matter of signposting professional help and checking in with that person until you know they are seeing either a counsellor or their GP.
>
> David believes that, unless businesses get better at dealing with mental health in the same way they deal with physical health, they will have increasing numbers of HRM issues to deal with and lose many more employees to long-term work-related stress. Businesses have to create kinder cultures for employees to feel they can break their silence and talk openly about their emotional well-being. David has committed the rest of his career to 'breaking the silence' that exists around mental health and creating stigma-free environments.

How do you feel about the explicit call to organisations to bring a full awareness of mental health and well-being into their tactical and strategic awareness? Do you think it the right thing to do? Is it possible?

In the future, what will managing people be about? Well, we can expect the following to feature (and also expect some surprises):

- lifestyle career choices
- gap years at all ages, not just between school and university
- lifelong learning
- a move from corporate social responsibility to a business model of sustainability (see Chapter 12)
- more interest in talent and succession management involving millennials
- a lot more virtual teamwork.

The last one on this list, teamwork, is a perennial MBA topic, second only to leadership as an object of scrutiny. From talking to executives about their experiences at work, my opinion is that organisations are cautious about the future. They will want managers who are confident with virtual working, willing to be flexible about how and when they work, and committed to putting their personal development goals on hold, if possible. Not great news for the self-directed, lifelong learner, who will be looking for balance between work and home. Technology will blur the lines between work and 'life' even more in the future, which means that building networks will be the key skill.

Teams: working with and through others

First-line managers will be expected to demonstrate a willingness to become part of them; middle managers a proficiency in leading them; senior managers a command of the subtleties of managing people in them. With increasingly flat management hierarchies and matrix reporting structures, teams and teamwork have become a ubiquitous feature of large organisations in the last 30 years. Even small to medium-sized enterprises (SMEs) often construct work around them. Teams and groups interest academics, too, and have been studied for decades. Influential psychologist Kurt Lewin coined the term 'group dynamics' in 1945, and the subject has filled the pages of management textbooks ever since.[8] Our study of group covers many scenarios, including a workplace team. All teams must have a specific reason (or charter) for their existence, but there are really two basic types:

1 **Collaborative:** any group whose aim is achievement of one shared goal or output; in other words, the output can be achieved only by working together.

2 **Cooperative:** any group whose aim is for everyone in it to reach their own goal; in other words, each person's goal is personal but will be reached more easily with the help or support of others.

Despite its popularity in organisational settings, the direct benefit of teamwork is hard to measure. In addition, teamwork is quite hard to get right. The model of group formation that has outlived most others is Bruce Tuckman's four-stage model, first developed in the 1950s and shown in Figure 4.2. Tuckman's language has entered management speak as shorthand for any group's theoretical navigation from first contact to task achievement. US management consultant Patrick Lencioni suggests that teams need to overcome five dysfunctions (each with a remedy):[9]

1 **Absence of trust:** team members need to be open to each other.

2 **Fear of conflict:** trust allows disagreement and questions.

3 **Lack of commitment:** early conflict and opinion sharing allows for genuine buy-in later on.

4 **Avoidance of accountability:** commitment allows teams to hold each other accountable for decisions and actions.

5 **Inattention to results:** overcoming all of the above lets the team focus on the charter (collective goal).

In the 1980s, Meredith Belbin concluded that an effective team needed a balance of different types of behaviours over the life of a project and that different people tended to prefer to play (or to prefer avoiding) a combination of nine team roles.[10] The nine roles are:

Implementer: being disciplined, reliable, conservative and efficient. Turning ideas into practical actions.

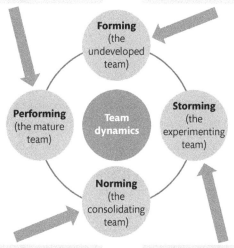

- Flexibility of approach
- Leadership decided by situation
- Commitment to team success
- Aware of principles/social aspects
- Rewarding and productive

- Feelings not dealt with
- Conformity
- Much talking, little listening
- Weaknesses/mistakes hidden
- No shared view of task
- Defensive against outside threats

Forming (the undeveloped team)

Performing (the mature team)

Team dynamics

Storming (the experimenting team)

Norming (the consolidating team)

- Confident but not complacent
- Willing to solve team problems
- Handle conflict constructively
- Follow agreed methods, not inflexible
- Interpersonal competence
- Learning and developing

- Review of methods
- Problems faced more openly
- More options considered
- Personal/group issues
- Temporarily more inward looking, more listening

FIGURE 4.2 Tuckman's stages of group development
Source: Adapted from Tuckman, B. (1965) 'Developmental sequence in small groups', *Psychological Bulletin*, 63(6): 384-99. Reproduced with permission of the American Psychological Association.

Team worker: being cooperative, mild, perceptive and diplomatic. Listening to avert friction.

Plant: being creative, imaginative and unorthodox. Solving difficult problems.

Resource investigator: being extrovert, enthusiastic and communicative. Exploring opportunities and developing contacts.

Shaper: being challenging, dynamic and thriving on pressure. Being courageous to overcome obstacles.

Coordinator: being mature, confident, a good chairperson. Clarifying goals, promoting decision making and delegating well.

Monitor evaluator: being sober, strategic and discerning. Seeing all options and judging accurately.

Completer-finisher: being painstaking and conscientious. Searching out errors or omissions and delivering on time.

Specialist: being single-minded, self-starting and dedicated. Providing task-specific knowledge and skills in rare supply.

Tuckman's theory and Belbin's work with management teams in the 1980s and 1990s are examples of the type of modelling of team processes used on MBA programmes. A high-performing team (HPT) is any group that achieves and then exceeds the goals it has been set while at the same time respecting and facilitating the individual objectives of its members. HPTs are difficult to build and even more difficult to maintain, and even Tuckman observed that teams frequently slipped back to earlier stages of formation and that the final 'performing' stage may be short-lived.

Is there anything wrong with this whole approach to teamwork? It might be said that managers often prefer the simple solution to the complex one, even when the complex is the more insightful. In other words, MBAs love shortcuts, academics like categorising the world and practitioners enjoy getting results. Theories about teamwork are rarely questioned critically in business schools and, while sometimes a shorthand rule of thumb can help, the reality is more complex.

Performance of the individual

Traditionally, performance has been about improving employee productivity through systems of motivation and reward, but this is a dynamic field that has changed enormously over the last 30 years in many parts of the world. Changes in legislation covering the rights and responsibilities of employers and employees, expectations of higher economic wealth and also of access to either full-, part-time or flexible working, as well as macroeconomic cycles of relative prosperity and austerity, have all influenced the pay and reward systems organisations use to manage performance.

This topic may appear in an organisation in the following ways:

▌ **Strategic:** as part of forward planning (and linked to strategy). In practice, many organisations see this as a cycle of activities and processes. It encompasses recruitment, reward and pay, generic training and development, pipeline, talent development and succession planning, and establishment of policies to monitor and maintain standards of process.

▌ **Tactical:** as part of regular or systematic reviews for individuals delivered usually by line management.

▌ **Ad hoc:** dealing with situations where something has gone wrong. Unfortunately, this is usually approached in terms of a need to fix the employee rather than a need to fix the system, even though, in the majority of cases, it is the context that is causing the issue. A great employee can be swallowed up in a poor system.

We've already seen that theories of motivation play a big part in understanding how to manage performance levels, but it remains a difficult concept to measure. Bonus cultures and corporate pension schemes have begun to face more criticism and restrictions, and reward systems in the future may need to find original and flexible mechanisms for remuneration.

> ### DAY BY DAY PRACTICE
>
> **1** What motivates you at work? What kind of psychological contract is there between you and your organisation?
>
> **2** What will be the main challenges in finding, recruiting and motivating staff in your organisation in coming years? You might want to discuss this with senior managers and HR.

Developing an HR strategy

In the previous chapter, I said that the operations function always has one eye on managing the present and the other on planning for the future. It should be the same when it comes to managing the people who run, organise and contribute to any organisation. The strategic side of managing people is about two things:

1 Making sure that the right human resources will be in place in the future. This future focus is strategic because it requires hedging against a scarcity of labour. In free-market economies, people are free to come and go and – despite constraints of political, social and economic circumstances – organisations must develop policies that will supply quality staff. Globally, the shortage of qualified personnel in the health sector, for example, is so acute that strategic HRM is often a governmental priority.

2 Negotiating the right systems of motivation, rewards and contractual control to meet the uncertainties of a contingent future, and of maintaining a balance in the tension between operating profitably while respecting the rights and responsibilities of employing people around the world.

Strategic HRM in the next 20 years will need to keep pace with the speed of change in other areas of business.

Putting it together: HR takes a Bath

One framework that brings all these messages together in one place and links them to strategy is the Bath model of people and performance, shown in Figure 4.3.[11] Concluded from in-depth studies of 12 different companies by a group of researchers based at Bath University, the model was an attempt to:

▌ understand the relationship between all the factors involved in a competitive and sustainable competitive advantage in HR strategy, and

▌ explain the motivational impact of 'discretionary' behaviours on performance.

The research revealed three things:

1 Organisations need to embody their 'big idea' in their HR practices. A clear sense of 'what we stand for' emerges in the relationships between the various elements.

2 Frontline managers are the ones who bring these relationships to life.

3 The 11 policies in the model all link to satisfaction, which links to performance, which in turn is linked to value. But different roles and levels in an organisation need different combinations of those policies.

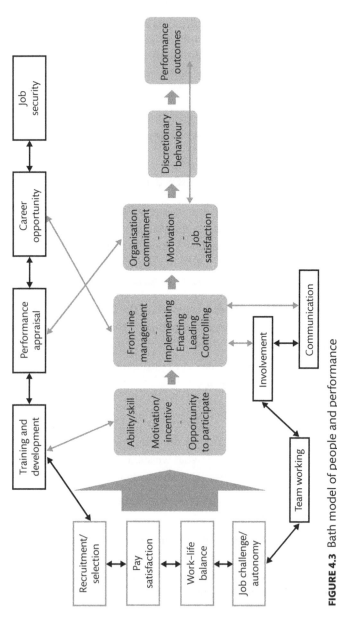

FIGURE 4.3 Bath model of people and performance

Source: Purcell, J., Kinnie, N., Hutchinson, S., Rayton, B. and Swart, J. (2003) 'Understanding the People and Performance Link: Unlocking the Black Box', with the permission of the Chartered Institute of Personnel and Development. London (**www.cipd.co.uk**)

The story of human resource management as a function first
went from study of structure to study of culture formed in the
structure. Now it is moving again from culture to a study of
the relation of culture and structure as a dynamic and open
system. The learning organisation is now a byword for good
management practice in managing people.

QUESTIONS FOR REFLECTION

1 How do you describe yourself? Does your job title also
function as your identity? If you had to give up your job
tomorrow, how would you describe yourself?

2 What sorts of things make you work harder than the
minimum?

Further reading

A classic text: *Toward A Psychology of Being*, by
Abraham Maslow (2010 reprint of
1962 edition 1st edition), Martino Fine
Books.

Going deeper: *Strategy and Human Resource
Management* by Peter Boxall and John
Purcell (4th edition, 2015), Palgrave
Macmillan. A comprehensive textbook,
pitched at the right level for MBAs and
mid-career managers.

Watch this: 'Drive', Dan Pink's engaging 2010 talk
on human motivation, animated by
the RSA.

Notes

1 Hofstede, G., Hofstede, G.J. and Minkov, M. (2010) *Cultures and Organizations: Software of the Mind*, 3rd edition, McGraw-Hill Professional.
2 Schein, E. (2010) *Organizational Culture and Leadership*, 4th edition, John Wiley & Sons.
3 Mintzberg, H. (1971) 'Managerial work: analysis from observation', *Management Science*, 18(2): B97–B110.
4 Peters, T. and Waterman, R. (2004) *In Search of Excellence: Lessons from America's Best-run Companies*, 2nd edition, Profile Books.
5 Herzberg, F., Mausner, B. and Snyderman, B. (1959) *The Motivation to Work*, 2nd edition, John Wiley.
6 Maslow, A.H. (1943) 'A theory of human motivation', *Psychological Review*, 50(4): 370–96.
7 www.breakingthesilence.co.uk.
8 Lewin, K. (1947) 'Frontiers in group dynamics. I. Concept, method and reality in social science; social equilibria', *Human Relations*, 1: 5–40.
9 Lencioni, P. (2002) *The Five Dysfunctions of a Team: A Leadership Fable*, John Wiley & Sons.
10 Belbin, M. (2010) *Team Roles at Work*, 2nd edition, Routledge.
11 Purcell, J., Kinnie, N., Hutchinson, S., Rayton, B. and Swart, J. (2003) *Understanding the People and Performance Link: Unlocking the Black Box*, Chartered Institute of Personnel and Development.

Finance 1: accounting
Reconciling numbers and decision making

> *Money is better than poverty, if only for financial reasons.*
>
> Woody Allen, *Without Feathers*

In a nutshell

This chapter covers the effective use of financial and economic data to support planning, control and decision making for value creation. It's a misconception (albeit a tempting one) that the job of an experienced chief financial officer (CFO) is to find a thousand different ways of saying no. A CFO's job is to agree robust ways of saying yes to value creation and their caution is usually because they are custodians of the resource that is our store and measure of value: money.

Accounting can be jargon-heavy and is highly regulated, but you do not need to know everything a CFO or accountant knows to work alongside the financial experts. When you understand something of the tools and principles of accounting and finance, it is directly applicable to the work you do and you will be better equipped to justify and defend your use of the organisation's resources to achieve its goals.

In this chapter you will:

▌ learn the difference between management and financial accounting

▌ study economic theory at the level of individuals and organisations

▌ understand the importance of the time value of money

▌ evaluate an organisation's performance using financial statements

The basis of accounting

Before diving into an alphabet soup of ratios and economic formulas, the best place to start is with what managers actually do day to day. Yours is a world of decisions and actions, but the logic behind many of an organisation's plans comes from economic theory. The language and practice of accounting are designed to measure the performance of decision making and so all the information provided in this view of accounting is historical. In other words, it comes from looking back. There are two broad areas of accounting:

▌ **Management accounting** has an internal audience. It is about the planning and decision making required to meet given objectives and is linked to microeconomic theory (the economics of individual actions). As a part of this, *cost accounting* establishes budgets linking detailed activities in the short-term future to various types of cost. Most managers are involved in preparing, managing and then tracking variances in budgets.

▌ **Financial accounting** uses data from past performance to analyse and interpret where you are in the present and to gauge the current viability of your business. Accounts have to be produced by all limited-liability companies. They summarise and consolidate all the activities from the last year and express them as numbers. Financial accounting thus presents the outcomes of the decisions made in management accounting in a way that is consistent and comparable. In *MBA Day by Day* we're going to use the published accounts of a major UK grocery retailer, Morrisons, to illustrate some of the main aspects of this part of accounting.

I will begin with management accounting, then look at financial accounting, in order to see in more detail the differences between them.

CASE STUDY

Morrisons supermarkets: introduction

With just over 11 per cent share of the UK grocery retail market, Morrisons is a FTSE 100 company and the fourth largest supermarket chain in a fiercely competitive sector where its closest competitors are Tesco, Sainsbury's and Asda (part of Wal-Mart). Founded in 1899, from its home base in the North of England, Morrisons expanded when it purchased the assets of its rival Safeway in 2008, doubling in size and gaining a nationwide network of superstores. Morrisons' value proposition is built around a vertically integrated supply chain (it owns all the farms and warehousing that supply its fresh produce) and an in-store format that is deliberately reminiscent of a traditional British high street or market.

Morrisons has 18 manufacturing sites, 9 distribution centres and 491 stores, most of which are on large, out-of-town sites. It lagged behind its competitors in moving to smaller, urban convenience stores, and experienced financial difficulties that led the senior management to launch a strategy called 'Fix, Rebuild and Grow' in 2015. The company says it is focusing on its customers, staff and traditional core supermarket strengths for long-term rather than short-term growth, but it has also grown its wholesale business dramatically, taking advantage of its strengths in supply chain management. ▶

> Under the stewardship of a new senior management team
> hired largely from rivals Tesco in 2015, after posting a
> £795 million loss on the back of a massive write-down on
> the book value of its properties, recent results have been
> positive. In 2018, the company paid dividends nearly double
> the previous year, and promises a sustainable dividend to
> shareholders. Yet the outlook in a volatile market and low
> margin sector is difficult, with increasing competition from
> discount supermarkets, consolidation among some of its
> major competitors, growth of rival online grocery shopping
> channels, and uncertainty over the effects of Brexit. Focusing
> on its traditional strengths and pulling back from ambitious
> expansion plans is balanced with selective innovation and
> partnerships, such as a 2016 agreement to house the UK's
> largest collection of Amazon Lockers in its supermarkets, as
> well as build grocery tie-ins with Amazon Prime and Pantry.

Management accounting

In buying this book, you made a decision. You incurred a
cost, which was balanced with an expectation of a benefit
that would be worth something in return. You could have
done other things with your money, so, the chances are you
weighed up any benefits relative to, for example, buying a
different book, or a meal, or perhaps using the money to pay
off a debt. That is a small example; a much bigger one could
be the cost of signing up for an MBA, which is why managers
often spend years thinking about it. Getting the most out
of limited resources is always an issue. In organisational
settings, when it's someone else's money, you need to show
judgement and rigour in the decisions you make because
usually they will have an effect on the bottom line.

Economic activities need to align with organisational
goals. Every organisation has limited resources – it can't
do everything and what it can do usually can't be done all
at once. Remembering the twin roles of management from

Chapter 1 (standing in place of the owners and the ethical creation of value), you begin to see – regardless of whether it's the monthly budget or 10-year capital expenditure – how financial information can help you move from being a re-active to a pro-active decision maker.

Management accounting employs concepts from business economics to help you decide on future courses of action that can be justified on managerial grounds, so let's begin there.

Microeconomic concepts

Economic theory tries to explain everything from macro levels of universal market forces through to the micro levels of what goes on inside an organisation. Economic theory influences tactical and strategic decisions on pricing, performance management, marketing and future investment. MBA programmes often look at this topic from a perspective that assumes rational decisions are made by self-interested individuals who are motivated to maximise efficiency for economic return.

Here are five key microeconomic concepts that are basic to an understanding of finance.

1 Scarcity and utility

The basis for what most organisations do is *scarcity*. Simply put, a demand is created as soon as people perceive a shortage of something. When this happens, choices have to be made, and there is a close relationship between choice and scarcity. In the rational view of the individual (or the firm), scarcity plus enlightened self-interest lead to decisions based on available information. Organisations not only try to identify what is scarce (and in demand), they also see whether they can limit it or add to it.

Utility is the level of expected satisfaction derived from a good or service. It might seem straightforward to expect that more of something provides greater satisfaction, but this is not so. Utility diminishes (the second sip is never as refreshing as the first).

2 Forms of competition

Perfect competition is a special (and theoretical) situation where there are enough buyers and sellers in a market – each with access to perfect information – that it is impossible for any single entity or party to influence the price, which is set in terms of the margin over the cost of production, not in terms of what others are charging. In perfect competition, demand drives down price only to a point where the threat of a new competitor is removed. A higher price would attract competition (i.e. it would be worth entering the market). A lower price is unprofitable. At this point, it meets the optimal supply at a rate that produces normal profit, or what it takes to keep the business a going concern. Normal profit needs to be considered as a cost because the price set at this point is the minimum expectation of return. Perfect competition doesn't really exist, but its consideration guides just about all investment decisions and policy or law regulating markets, especially utilities.

The opposite of perfect competition is *monopoly*, another largely theoretical state where a dominant player supplies at a price of cost plus margin unrestricted by competition. Many markets operate as *oligopolies*, where there is limited competition between a few suppliers that are dominant in the market. These competing organisations tend to be of roughly the same size and will tend to act reactively and proactively in regard to competitors. The interdependence among players is what makes an oligopoly special and this drives strategic analysis and planning among ***profit-maximising*** firms. Oligopolies are often the subject of mathematical modelling of two theoretical players using **game theory**. However, there are almost no examples of monopolies that aren't regulated.

3 Costs and revenue

Revenue (or turnover) is defined by the effective demand in the market × price. *Costs* are dictated by the price paid for inputs (materials, labour and capital) and the efficiency in management of processes needed to transform them to outputs. A marginal cost is the change in total cost that results from the production of one extra unit. If costs for inputs are known, the total cost can be calculated. Microeconomics also recognises the opportunity cost of choosing one course of action over another.

4 Supply and demand curve

Supply and demand curves (see Figure 5.1) are lines plotted on a graph on axes of price (P) versus quantity (Q) and illustrate that:

▮ demand (D) is the ratio of how many or how much of a good or service a customer is willing to buy at a given price. The lower the price, the more the customers will want (in theory), though it matters also what alternatives are available and how much money you have to spend

▮ supply (S) is the ratio between the given price a supplier of a good or service must charge to cover costs and make a margin and the quantity that it can supply at that price. The higher the price, the more it can make or supply.

Demand curves slope downwards while supply curves slope up. At some point, these two theoretical lines meet in equilibrium where supply and demand are matched by what buyer and seller are willing to accept in price. When there is more demand for something than there is supply, a shortage results and, generally, the price will go up.

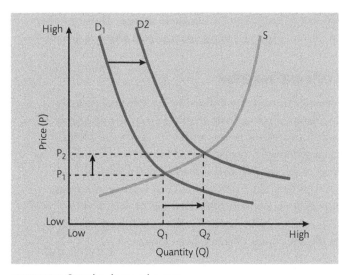

FIGURE 5.1 Supply–demand curve

Similarly, where there is an excess of supply, the price tends to reduce. Getting the supply side of this equation correct is crucial for many businesses and organisations, and this is often the primary goal of operations managers. Elasticity is the sensitivity between variables in a supply and demand relationship. The ratio between a change in a price and the demand for it is called the elasticity of demand. Inelastic is if you put the price up (or down) and demand stays about the same.

5 Economic profit (EP)

Economic profit is a way of measuring the effectiveness of how resources are used. As a part of goal setting, evaluation of performance, capital budgeting and valuation it can be very important. Value is derived by subtracting cost of capital from net operating profit over a given period. EVA, or economic value added, is one way to show how much wealth has been generated and is an alternative to budgeted targets. It works only with accounting centres that are responsible for their own income, but can link several centres to track performance overall.

Costs and benefits

Decisions always need to be made about the best use of
scarce resources. At some point, the costs and benefits of
your decisions will be assessed and measured beyond what
was set out in a budget. One of the best ways of doing this is
by calculating and comparing future marginal or additional
costs and benefits resulting from a decision. Even if you
have only one choice in mind, the comparison between that
and what would happen if you just left things as they are
can help.

For the purposes of most business or management
decisions, the future is converted into a relationship
between time and the value of money. It is no simple matter
to measure every type of future benefit in money terms.
Some of this is driven by an understanding of the concepts
of demand and of supply, which will always incur a cost to
make happen. There is a great deal of debate in accounting
on the language of costs, but the most important principle
to keep in mind is knowing which sorts are relevant to
your decision making and which are not. The most basic
division is between fixed costs (which don't change with
increases or decreases in activity) and variable costs (which
change in direct proportion to activity). Typically, tactical
decision making involves using a set of assumptions
to adjust capacity to meet demand and then modelling
changes in variable costs to identify the break-even point
(also known as cost-volume-profit analysis, or CVP). There
is always an opportunity cost incurred, if only because
the time used in one activity cannot then also be used to
generate value in another.

Another important aspect of this is whether an organisation
is better off paying outside contractors or bringing work
inside, often known as the make-or-buy decision. Make or
buy decisions are strategic and significant.

Future cash flows and net present value

Short-term decision analysis requires the following steps:

▌ Define the problem requiring a decision.

▌ Make a thorough list of alternative courses of action.

▌ Identify and discard alternatives that do not deserve closer analysis.

▌ Calculate the financial cost–benefit differences of the remaining choices.

▌ Weigh up the financial and non-financial factors to make a decision.

Longer term, options for growing or for development that do not rely on external sources of funding require an extension of managerial decision making beyond budgets. Finance now begins to resemble investment and, although the basic principles are the same as for short-term spending, there are several tools that a manager needs to know about to evaluate the different options open to them.

The most important consideration, bearing in mind the focus on value, is knowing the effect of any investment on future performance – whether replacing worn-out assets, cutting back on costs, funding internal expansion or reacting to external conditions. Most managers will not have direct responsibility for sourcing or appraising capital expenditure, but are fully involved in justifying, preparing and delivering such projects. It helps to know that the main financial criteria for justification of investment projects are that they:

▌ are in line with the objectives of the organisation

▌ will produce a return that exceeds the financing cost over their economic lifetime

▌ are the best choice financially among all those available, including their residual value at the end of the project.

Assuming that you can work out the future cash flows and predict the many variables that could affect this, how do you work out what's the best way to invest in a project?

The simplest method, payback period, compares the initial capital outlay for each option under consideration and calculates how long, in years, it will take to recover that original investment, and then how far into the expected economic life of the project this payback occurs. Payback is simple, but is unadjusted in that it ignores the time value of money (this is the fundamental idea in finance that money in the present is preferable to the same amount in the future). Techniques that factor in the value of the rate of return (or return on investment, ROI) over the whole economic life of the project need to adjust to this.

A commonly used technique to calculate the value of the various investment choices over a period of time longer than one year is net present value (NPV). If the present value of future benefits can be shown to exceed the present value of future costs, the project should be undertaken as it will add value to the organisation. Discounting is the process of finding the current value of future cash flows when they have been adjusted for future interest or inflation. At what rate to discount usually will be a given and is termed the cost of capital. Any project meeting this hurdle rate will, in theory, end up adding value.

Budgeting and budgets

An important sign of career progression is budgeting responsibility, so nearly all managers seek it. Actual budget preparation and appraisal can be the cause of much stress at work so it's worth looking at the distinction between the process and the product:

▌ **Budgeting** is a process to forecast the appropriate allocation, control and use of resources. It is often cultural, political and idiosyncratic (i.e. how one organisation goes about it is likely to be different from others). Budgeting cycles can be lengthy and expensive. For example, the Ford Motor Company spends in excess of $1 billion each year just on its budgeting process. For some, budgeting is an area of controversy because it is seen as being old-fashioned and out of touch with the fluid, project-based structures found in many companies.

▌ **A budget** is an approved plan that quantifies in monetary terms and over a fixed period an organisation's future activities. Because a budget predicts, it can be used as a control mechanism by prompting explanation of any difference or variance between the plan and the actual. Budgets may be incremental (new activities receive new funds), zero-based (each new round assumes activities are being done for the first time), rolling (ongoing process of adding a new accounting period when the current one has expired) or flexible (designed to be adjusted to suit changes in activities).

DAY BY DAY PRACTICE

1 Speak to your finance director. Ask them how they have changed their budgeting in the last three or four years.

2 How do they think the budgeting process could be improved in your organisation? How would any of those changes affect or involve you?

Budget variance and approval are day-to-day features that will be found in all organisations. The largest operating cost for many firms relates to people, but using budgets to manage staff performance is risky. Where this happens, managing variance produces short-term or self-interested thinking and becomes a stress on people.

Fluency in accounting should matter to you because it will help answer questions that go beyond how things are going compared with the plan. This is important because, as a senior manager, you will always need to answer four questions:

1 Do we have enough cash to pay the bills and remain viable?

2 How are we doing compared with our competitors?

3 Are we better or worse off than we were in the past?

4 What will our financial position be at a given time in the future?

DAY BY DAY PRACTICE

1 Describe the relationship you have with your finance team during the budgeting cycle. Who is responsible for explaining any variance in your budget: you, your finance managers, or a combination?

2 What assumptions about budgeting have been used in your organisation?

To reach conclusions and understand the effective use of these and other accounting principles, you must know something about using financial statements to produce financial ratios.

Financial accounting

The audience in financial accounting are people outside your organisation with an interest in how it is performing (whether you are creating value). Because companies with publicly traded shares must publish their audited accounts in annual reports, we are able to examine their statements for the story behind the performance. Looking at the three financial statements from the 2016–17 accounts of Morrisons

plc should provide a few clues to the decision making in
the company around its tactical and strategic position in the
market. Remember, the notes section of the annual report
contains information to help you read the statements, as
well as a lot of the company detail and background the
consolidated numbers cannot show you.

Financial statements

All organisations must ensure access to cash, even when
making a profit and especially when that business is new
or has invested in non-current assets (e.g. equipment,
vehicles and buildings that the organisation plans to own
for more than one year). So, first, we need to understand the
significance of the cash flow statement, not least because a
lack of liquidity is the single most frequent reason businesses
fail. See Table 5.1.

The cash flow statement is a common-sense record of
actual (as opposed to booked) inflows and outflows of
cash over a period, showing start and end cash balances. A
cash flow forecast is the same, but for a future period. The
advantage of this is that it enables management to adjust
to future shortfalls in liquidity, either by sourcing funds
temporarily to cover the cash shortfall or by speeding
up the arrival of revenues and delaying outgoings from
business activities.

The cash flow statement consolidates income from three
sets of activities: operating, investing and financing.
For Morrisons (see the following) this shows that cash
from operating activities has fallen to £884 million from
the previous year's £1.1 million. It is worth looking at
Morrisons' annual report to see what the company says is
behind this drop. It could be that its increased sales have,
for example, forced Morrisons to increase its working

capital to build stock and tie funds up with debtors, which would make sense. The other explanation could be inefficiencies with how the company's management make decisions, though there is reasonable evidence that their turnaround strategy is proving effective

The income statement, or profit and loss (P&L), covers the period of time between two balance sheets but, unlike the cash flow, is not dependent on whether money has been received or spent yet (not only are 'profit' and 'cash' different concepts, but profit is multi-layered and potentially confusing as a comparable measure). Table 5.2 shows the Morrisons 2018 P&L.

The P&L is a retrospective (and statutory) annual income statement that shows the balance of revenue (turnover) less any direct cost of sales. This gives you the gross profit, from which all other expenses, such as wages, overheads, dividends and due taxation, are deducted, leaving the net profit (the infamous bottom line). The P&L is the most important measurement with input to strategy because it is what organisations use to measure themselves against their competition.

TABLE 5.1 Consolidated cash flow statement for Morrisons plc, 2017–18

	2018 (£ m)	2017 (£ m)
Cash flows from operating activities		
Cash generated from operations	**884**	1,113
Interest paid	**(66)**	(100)
Taxation paid	**(74)**	(35)
Net cash inflow from operating activities	**744**	978

▶

	2018 (£ m)	2017 (£ m)
Cash flows from investing activities		
Interest received	**4**	6
Dividends received from joint venture	**8**	8
Proceeds from the sale of investments	**-**	(44)
Proceeds from sale of property, plant and equipment	**108**	79
Purchase of property, plant and equipment, investment and assets classified as held-for-sale	**(429)**	(374)
Purchase of intangible assets	**(71)**	(45)
Net cash outflow from investing activities	**(380)**	(282)
Cash flows from financing activities		
Purchase of own shares for trust	**(4)**	(5)
Settlement of employee tax liability for share awards	**(7)**	–
Proceeds from exercise of employee share options	**33**	–
Proceeds on settlement of derivative financial instruments	**6**	37
Repayment of borrowings	**(245)**	(729)
Costs incurred on repayment of borrowings	**(17)**	(42)
Dividends paid	**(129)**	(118)

	2018 (£ m)	2017 (£ m)
Net cash outflow from financing activities	**(363)**	(857)
Net increase/decrease in cash and cash equivalents	**1**	(161)
Cash and cash equivalents at start of period	**326**	487
Cash and cash equivalents at end of period	**327**	326

Source: **www.morrisons-corporate.com**

TABLE 5.2 Consolidated income statement for Morrisons plc, 2017–18

	2018 (£ m)	2017 (£ m)
Turnover	**17,262**	16,317
Cost of sales	**(16,629)**	(15,713)
Gross profit	**633**	604
Other operating income	**78**	76
Profit/loss on disposal and exit of properties and sales of investments	**19**	32
Administrative expenses	**(272)**	(244)
Operating profit	**458**	468
Finance costs	**(94)**	(160)
Finance income	**14**	15
Share of profit of joint venture (net of tax)	**2**	2

▶

	2018 (£ m)	2017 (£ m)
Profit before taxation	380	337
Taxation	**(69)**	(20)
Profit for the period attributable to the owners of the company	311	305
Other comprehensive expense for the period, net of tax	245	105
Total comprehensive income for the period attributable to the owners of the company	556	410

Source: **www.morrisons-corporate.com**

The income statement might give an indication of just how competitive this sector is. It shows increased revenue from £16.3 million to £17.3 but gross profit as a percentage of this has not increased quite in line (3.7% for 2017, 3.66% for 2018), which hints at margins under pressure.

Dividends as earnings per share (EPS) are calculated on profit attributable to the owners of the company, which at £311 million is slightly up on the previous year but the margin squeeze and increase in administrative expenses have eaten into the increased revenue figures.

The balance sheet will show the good news, or the bad news, about what a business owns now compared with a year ago (see Table 5.3). What you see is a slice through the organisation on a given day. It's rather like a snapshot, or freeze frame, and – like many individuals who know they are going to be photographed – organisations will try to look their best on that date. This is certainly true for large companies that need to reassure investors or owners that they are creating value.

TABLE 5.3 Consolidated balance sheet for Morrisons plc, 2017–18

	2018 (£ m)	2017 (£ m)
Assets		
Non-current assets		
Goodwill and intangible assets	428	445
Property, plant and equipment	7,243	7,227
Investment property	33	33
Pension asset	612	293
Investments in joint venture	53	56
	8,385	8,070
Current assets		
Stocks	686	614
Debtors	250	214
Derivative financial assets	15	22
Cash and cash equivalents, other financial assets	327	326
Assets classified as held-for-sale	4	-
	1,282	1,176
Liabilities		
Current liabilities		
Creditors	(2,981)	(2,837)
Short-term borrowings	(72)	-
Derivative financial liabilities	(13)	(3)

	2018 (£ m)	2017 (£ m)
Current tax liabilities	**(15)**	(24)
	(3,081)	(2,864)
Non-current liabilities		
Borrowings	**(1,245)**	(1,550)
Derivative financial liabilities	**(1)**	(5)
Pension liability	**(18)**	(21)
Deferred tax liabilities	**(478)**	(417)
Provisions	**(299)**	(326)
	(2,041)	(2,319)
Net assets	**4,545**	4,063
Shareholders' equity		
Called-up share capital	**236**	234
Share premium	**159**	128
Capital redemption reserve	**39**	39
Merger reserve	**2,578**	2,578
Retained earnings and hedging service	**1,533**	1,084
Total equity attributable to the owners of the company	**4,454**	4,063

Source: **www.morrisons-corporate.com**

The balance in a balance sheet is between what the company owns versus what it owes to third parties and shareholders. There are different ways of expressing this equation, for example Morrisons deducts liabilities from assets and then balances the result with what is owed to shareholders, but the basic formula is:

$$total\ assets = total\ liabilities$$

Assets are those resources owned by the business that can be represented in monetary terms and that are expected to be used in some way for economic benefit. Current assets include the working capital (anything 'liquid' or available in the short term to generate value), while fixed assets are those items that the organisation owns and that will have an expected economic life of more than one year.

On the other side, liabilities show where the organisation has a monetary obligation to others. This will include any loans outstanding as well as the capital invested by the shareholders, or reserves such as retained profits from past years.

As for Morrisons, if liquidated, the balance sheet shows a book value of £4,545 million because this is, in effect, the amount liable to the shareholders. This is based on accounting rules and principles and is not the same as what its investors in the Stock Market might achieve, and the share price is set by many other factors as well. However, you can see that this is more than the previous year so, arguably, the course the company is taking in terms of realigning the business is going well and is in line with the increase in profits from the previous year.

Financial ratios

Ratios work by expressing one thing (e.g. profit) in relation to another (e.g. total assets) in order to provide useful **heuristic** information for decision making. It is not difficult to calculate ratios with the right data; the art lies in how you make sense of the results. But there are a great many key ratios, even at a high level, and too many to list in detail. The main categories are indicated below:

Profitability ratios: these look at earnings (profit) before interest and taxation as a percentage of total assets. Generally, the higher the ratio, the better the indicator of how much value the business is generating from its assets, but much depends on what is normal for that type of sector, or between similar competitors.

Liquidity, or working capital ratios: ('Can we pay our way?') It has already been mentioned that a business or organisation that has no cash available is not going to remain a going concern for very long. Liquidity ratios look at the way working capital cycles through a business.

Gearing, or leverage ratios: the two principal sources of financing a venture are shareholder equity and loans. The global recession that began in 2008 showed how access to short- and long-term loans is fundamental to businesses' growth and development. It is true that loans normally carry an interest obligation but, unlike dividends paid to shareholders, loans often benefit from the 'tax shield' and are deductible from tax. There is often an advantage in managing the relative amounts of debt from different sources. The relationship between debt and equity is called gearing.

Productivity ratios: an interesting use of financial ratios, though one that makes sense only in comparison with other factors, is to derive how much value is being provided by the human resource (nearly always an organisation's biggest cost).

Investor ratios: finally, and frequently quoted for publicly traded companies, some specific ratios are used for investor decision making.

Ratios are something of a minefield for MBA students because they come alive through calculation and interpretation in a context. On the page, they remain rather superficial. Because different organisations calculate and use them in different ways, it usually makes sense to get to know the ones that inform your industry, sector or company.

DAY BY DAY PRACTICE

1 Visit **http://www.annualreports.com/HostedData/ AnnualReports/PDF/LSE_MRW_2018.pdf** to access the 2018 accounts, or **http://markets.ft.com/research/ Markets/Tearsheets/Summary?s=MRW:LSE** for the FT's snapshot. Take some time to review the financial statements and accompanying notes, paying attention to which ratios it uses to report its financial KPIs.

2 Speak with the finance team in your organisation. See which financial ratios are important to your business and ask how they are calculated.

Putting it together: it all adds up

Accounting is a universal language, but it is spoken in many different accents and dialects. Practice varies not just among companies but from sector to sector and country to country. The presence of external regulation and standardisation in accounting means that everyone has a platform for comparison to look at their performance, but an organisation's internal financial decision making will constantly evolve. The use of numbers, ratios and mathematics in managerial accounting doesn't mean skills of interpretation or judgement aren't required; on the contrary, deriving meaning from numbers is the craft of doing business. Managers and leaders require answers to certain fundamental questions – ranging from whether we have enough cash available to pay our bills and stay in business, whether our shareholders are better off than a year ago, whether we're outperforming our competitors, and whether we need to find or free up financial resources in the future (this final point will be addressed in Chapter 8). Financial and management accounting provide these, and more.

QUESTIONS FOR REFLECTION

1. What does money mean to you?
2. Reflect on your career ambitions. What level of financial support or reward do you require to achieve your goals?

Further reading

A classic text: *Intelligent Investor: The Definitive Book on Value Investing – a Book of Practical Counsel* by Benjamin Graham (2006), Collins Business. First published in 1949 and on Warren Buffett's list of top three books about finance.

Going deeper: *Accounting and Finance for Non-Specialists* by Peter Atrill and Eddie McLaney (10th edition, 2017), Pearson.

                         Principles of Business Economics by Joseph Nellis and David Parker (2nd edition, 2006), Financial Times/ Prentice Hall.

Visit this: 'Beyond Budgeting Institute': **www.bbrt.org**. Dedicated to the sharing of best practice among organisations in planning and budgeting.

part

3

Strategic MBA thinking: how to manage the big picture

Strategy n. ['strætɪdʒi/] a plan of action to achieve a long-term goal, overall aim or desired end result

n your organisation, there are some things that are under your control and other things that are not. Those elements you can directly influence and that push you forward may be called *strengths*, and those that restrain you *weaknesses*. Those that lie outside your control but could be used to your advantage are *opportunities*, and what you can't control but what could restrict you are *threats*. These are the components of a SWOT analysis (see Figure P3.1). SWOT came out of the failure of long-range corporate planning in the USA in the 1960s and 1970s and still typifies the sort of summary framework applied to strategic decision and policy making today.

The 'internal–external' dichotomy of a SWOT is an example of a compelling idea in strategic thinking which we will

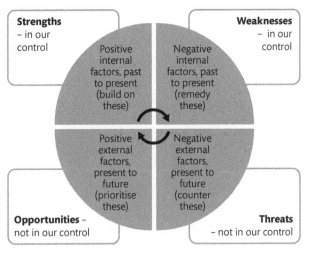

FIGURE P3.1 SWOT analysis

explore in this part. Strategic thinking is about making informed, intelligent choices from a set of considerations that extends beyond the boundaries, resources or culture of the organisation. Another way of looking at this is to say that strategy deals with what could be done in the future, and this future depends on the environment outside the organisation. But nothing in management is neat and tidy, and strategic thinking requires managers to shift how they see the world.

Strategic thinking involves:

▌ understanding the delicate relationship between an organisation and its environment

▌ setting and communicating the goals and ensuring the survival of the organisation through value creation

▌ undertaking medium- to long-term planning and making a small number of (relatively) irreversible decisions

▌ keeping a cool head under pressure and learning from mistakes.

Strategic thinking in the early stages for any organisation is relatively simple. But, as they grow and age, businesses develop more complex relationships with their internal and external environments. In particular, they become more sophisticated regarding their customers. Or they should do. But this requires a shift in management thinking beyond tactical decisions (these remain important) to ones that deal with new and unpredictable variables. The cost of misjudgement may be high. In late 2018, for example, the 134-year-old US department store chain and mail-order giant Sears, Roebuck and Co. (Sears) filed for Chapter 11 bankruptcy, having gone from 1st to 31st largest retailer in the USA. After being bought by Kmart in 2004, Sears had pursued a strategy of taking assets off its balance sheet to fund expansion online, but, by early 2017 it carried $4.2 billion in debt, considerably larger than its market capitalisation at the time.

There are four business areas associated with strategic thinking:

▌ marketing

▌ strategy

▌ corporate finance and governance

▌ global and international business.

We will see, in turn, how each of these is organised and how important it becomes to understand the language used to express ideas, concepts and theories at this level.

6

Marketing
Satisfying customer needs, profitably

The purpose of business is to create a customer.

Peter Drucker

In a nutshell

Marketing is about value as it is perceived by the customer. Every organisation has a customer because no organisation exists for long without demand for what it does. If demand changes, so must the organisation. In the eyes of your customer 'value' is not just about economics or functional needs, it is a connection to psychological desires and emotions, too.

In fact, some would even say that marketing is an all-encompassing philosophy of business. Marketing faculties at business schools tend to agree.

In this chapter you will:

▌ trace the history and development of marketing

▌ identify various marketing strategies available to organisations

▌ define brand and examine the importance of relationships with customers

▌ highlight how marketing happens between businesses

The value proposition

Marketing is the first MBA subject that explicitly moves between the internal and external environments of an organisation. Every organisation, whether multinational business, giant public institution, local charity or small start-up, will find marketing is the relevant perspective for setting levels of quality, service and price – the main components of the value proposition. This means that marketing is concerned first with identifying perceptions of value in the marketplace and then with the development, production and distribution of goods and services.

The tactical, practical and day-to-day business of marketing involves the implementation of projects and plans linked to the sale or advertising of what an organisation does. This is the domain of marketing as process and functional specialism. But the manager (and MBA student) should take a broader, strategic view that goes well beyond the marketing department.

Marketing is attuned to the way that the world – and the nature of competition – is changing. This makes it an exciting field of study with many stories and variants of application, but also a difficult one to define or keep completely up to date with.

DAY BY DAY PRACTICE

1 Who is the person in charge of marketing in your organisation? What are the activities and responsibilities of this person? Ask them whether their marketing spend went up or down in the last five years. Ask for the reasoning behind their responses.

2 Who are your organisation's customers? What would you say is the value proposition of your company? (Think in terms of quality, service and price as perceived by your customers.

A (very) brief history of marketing

The Chartered Institute of Marketing gives its definition of marketing as:

> the management process responsible for identifying, anticipating and satisfying customer requirements profitably.[1]

In 1960, a former executive of Pillsbury (a fast-moving consumer goods (FMCG) company), Robert Keith, summed up the development of marketing management in three ages:[2]

1. **The production era:** following an explosion of mass-production techniques (the Ford Model T assembly line is the archetypal example), the marketing task was to find ways to produce as much as possible as cheaply as possible. The focus was on profit from volume. Some have characterised this as the period before marketing, though this is not representative. Companies have engaged with their markets for centuries.

2. **The sales era; 'selling what we can make':** in the boom years after the Second World War there was a change. Supply began to outstrip demand and, as competitors were able to apply the same production techniques, marketing shifted to finding innovative ways of persuading customers to buy the surplus of goods being produced.

3. **The marketing era; 'making what we can sell':** from the 1960s on, companies switched to first understanding what the customer wants, then satisfying those needs (profitably). This may seem obvious, and some argue that it was like this all along, but it was not sophisticated and big business had grown physically and psychologically away from the end user. In this era, money was poured into finding new customers. The focus was now on market research to collect information about consumers

and competition, and processes for constant innovation for value creation.

Competitive advantage

The assumption of the marketing era is that others will try to be in the same space as you and will compete for market share by meeting the demands of your customers. This gives customers choice, which our economic system firmly believes to be a good thing, and has led to organisations becoming very, very interested in what strategies competitors are using. From this, we get to the concept of competitive advantage, an idea proposed most firmly by Michael Porter in the 1980s that you should look at which resources and abilities within your organisation lead to performance at a *higher* level than your competitors (more about this in Chapter 7).[3] This has proved to be a powerful idea in shaping corporate behaviour.

Porter's view has found some opposition. First, there is the argument that marketing has only ever had one era – that of putting the customer first. Second, that this is a rather narrow model that does not match the complexity of the post-internet world.

Much has changed since the 1980s and 1990s and there's now a fourth marketing phase:

4 **The relationship era:** this wants the whole organisation to have a market orientation, where market research is aligned to the internal functions (including relationships with suppliers) and all levels of management are asked to embrace marketing principles across the organisation. There are two specific things that have helped define this new marketing:

(a) a strategic focus on customer retention

(b) the internet has led to a redefining of consumer power and a fragmenting of traditional marketing domains.

Digital marketing, in particular, has challenged many organisations to think again. In fact, social media has already had an enormous impact on marketers and digital marketing may one day need a whole chapter in its own right. Maintaining a consistent message is a much greater challenge in an age where users can generate their own content on, for example, Twitter, Instagram or Facebook, access almost any provider on their smartphone and share instant feedback and complaints.

Marketing in business schools has been dominated by one name: Philip Kotler. His book, *Marketing Management*, has been a mainstay on MBA courses for many years.[4] With an emphasis on the societal role of marketing, it is a comprehensive overview of a transformation from the marketing orientation to the relationship era. Kotler's work has highlighted the various ways of looking at marketing in terms of strategy.

Marketing strategies

A market orientation is meaningless without a coordinated strategy behind it. Michael Porter, again, has been influential in this regard by outlining three generic strategies for competitive advantage, each with roots in a different era in marketing:

1. **Cost leadership:** by minimising your costs, you are able either to lower price or boost margin, so this is a strategy aimed at profitability. There are obvious links here to Chapter 3 and how operations are organised, and to Chapter 5 and how financing is managed. Strategic decisions are required in order to have a lower cost base than your competitors because the scale needed to achieve this may require considerable capital investment.

2. **Differentiation:** in the end, this can be judged only in the mind of the customer and assumes access to the right

information for them to know, or think they know, how your offering stands out. Differentiation may be real in the sense of features unique to your offering, or the result of careful promotion and branding.

3 **Focus:** this means finding a niche and concentrating only on that (at least to begin with). The niche may be a particular need or segment, and the growth of the internet has made it possible to reach previously difficult-to-get-to areas. A niche is sometimes a double-edged sword in business.

DAY BY DAY PRACTICE

1 Is the marketer's definition of value in conflict with the finance manager's (Chapter 5)? Are these aligned with the view of the CEO (Chapter 1)? What about the shareholder?

2 Economic value can be derived either from the production end (costs) or the consumption end (price) of the value chain. At which end of the spectrum does your organisation place most of its energy?

Porter's influence is slowly fading, partly because the business world he was describing has become more fragmented. Let's examine how someone else has perceived this. The six markets framework was devised by Adrian Payne at Cranfield University and is an example of an analytical tool for market orientation (see Figure 6.1). Keeping the 'classic' customer in the centre of things, it extends marketing to other domains, such as suppliers (this is sometimes called reverse marketing), recruiters of talent, and the potential contained in referrals from existing customers and agents or other intermediaries. An analysis is then made of any gaps or changes between past, current and future focus in the organisation.

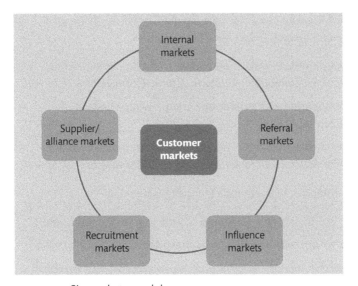

FIGURE 6.1 Six markets model
Source: Payne, A., Ballantyne, D. and Christopher, M. (2005) 'A stakeholder approach to relationship marketing strategy: The development and use of the "six markets' model"', *European Journal of Marketing*, 39(7/8): 855–71. Reproduced with permission of Emerald Group Publishing Ltd.

This still leaves plenty of open questions and opportunities. What is the market definition of what you do? Is it better to lead or follow others in the market? What are the things under the control of the organisation and what are the things outside (remember SWOT)? What are you doing with the direct contact you now have with your customers?

Segmentation, targeting and positioning

Limited resources and competitors in the same space mean organisations have to identify groups of customers with similar needs and similar expectations of a value proposition. This is called segmentation, but there are many ways of slicing up a potential market. Below are a few examples:

▌ **geographic:** by particular region or district, urban versus rural, or populations living in different climates

▌ **demographic:** by gender, age group, income bracket, educational level

▌ **psychographic:** by social class, social aspirations, values, behaviours, lifestyle choices and attitudes to value.

An attractive segment for a company is one that:

▌ is in line with the long-term objectives of the organisation

▌ is within reach using resources available

▌ has the potential to grow and be of a size that will sustain a profitable return.

Thorough identification of all the segments in the market will allow selection of those worth targeting. Targeting may also be subdivided into various decisions between differentiation and concentration within the segment. The ultimate goal for an organisation is to target customers one to one and, in some markets this sort of bespoke service is possible. Most companies, however, need to think carefully about the third step, positioning, where a detailed understanding of emotion, attitude and beliefs as drivers of value perception becomes crucial. Positioning statements connect the resources in an organisation to the segment it is targeting. They are expressions of how you want to be seen through the eyes of your customers. The world's longest-running positioning ad was the 25-year campaign for Swedish vodka brand Absolut – which began and used the distinctive bottle shape and sequence of generative verbal associations of its name in an ad campaign in 1980. This moved a local brand from obscurity to international fame and commercial success. It was a tactical move that became a strategic choice.

The link to the tactical: from the four to the seven Ps

The four Ps of marketing, developed by E. Jerome McCarthy in the 1960s, have now attained seminal status in marketing management.[5] For the record, they are:

▌**Product:** different eras have developed the idea of the product from 'what we make' to 'what needs making'. In theory, this is a constantly shifting issue and few organisations can keep on making the same thing without adjustments, innovation or reinvention. The customer has to be able to see the value for them of what your company does and this is the core benefit.

▌**Price:** for you, price is revenue, not cost (all other marketing Ps entail cost). To your customer, your price is a cost of their time, effort or money. A market orientation equates the value of a thing with what the customer is willing to pay for it. There are many considerations behind what price to set and profit is only one of them. Price, for example, may also establish your value position vis à vis your competitors. How you identify the features of your product as benefits for your customers may also be important.

▌**Place:** this used to be a very obvious matter of naming channels and locations for purchase. Availability in an increasingly interconnected and online world, even for tangible goods and traditional services, is more complex. The logistics of delivering and displaying your offering are critical to your customer's perception of value to them and, if they see a better alternative, unless you have a strong brand loyalty, they will move.

▌**Promotion:** communication with your customers (which, by the way, is also communication with your competitors) includes branding, advertising, public relations and gaining the attention of others with a consistent message. Increasingly, these channels are now set up as a form of two-way communication and collection of market data.

Academics and thinkers find it hard to resist alliteration, and the original four have since been expanded to reflect the importance in globalised economies of service industries:

▌ **People:** Chapter 4 highlighted the crucial role that human resources play in the success of any organisation, and contact points with customers will, almost certainly, include a personal element (or will need one when things don't go well). By including people in the marketing mix, you are saying that training, attitude and consistent service or support are as important as any other element.

▌ **Process:** many processes are not designed with the customer in mind, so this P is often overlooked. It is added in recognition that the customer experience of any process that delivers your offering is crucial to retention and reputation. Having to wait, not being kept informed and not being treated with respect – all can have a devastating effect on the bottom line (later in this chapter we look at this again as reputation).

▌ **Physical evidence:** making the intangible service feel more tangible is incredibly important for marketers. In some ways, this relates to 'place', above, but extends to include, for example, word-of-mouth testimonials of others, awards and certificates of excellence, and pre-purchase access to others who are already customers.

This palette in the marketing mix is an attractive framework to organise basic ideas, but is under severe pressure when you try to use it to keep up with the fragmented and rapidly changing consumer environment. How easily can you apply these to Google, iTunes or Facebook without presenting their business models as simplistic, or – in theory – wrong?

The shift from product to brand

The placement of a financial value of a company's brand (often found in financial statements) can potentially backfire on marketing. On the one hand, it raises the status and profile of the marketing function and enables budget allocation of funds to marketing activities but, on the other, it remains very difficult to know the effect of marketing spend on the bottom line. In a business or organisation with few physical assets, value is also derived from the perceived reputation, of which the brand is usually the major component. The Coca-Cola Company owns relatively few tangible assets other than production of the all-important concentrate, and it is estimated that at least 50 per cent of its market capitalisation is derived just from the premium of the brand name and bottling contracts. For McDonald's, the comparable figure is 70 per cent.[6]

DAY BY DAY PRACTICE

1 What are some of your favourite brands? What do those choices say about you?

2 How do you define your 'personal brand'? What are you most known for where you work?

Brands can resonate across generations. Keeping older, loyal consumers happy while also reaching out to the next generation is no easy task. Take a look below at how one of the world's leading toy companies has responded to this challenge.

CASE STUDY

Lego in the digital age

Few brands have gained the kind of loyalty over successive generations of consumers as has the family-owned Danish toy company Lego. Starting in 1932 with wooden toys, and ▶

producing its first, iconic, eight-studded plastic interlocking brick in 1947, over the years Lego has been both the world's most profitable toy-maker and on the verge of bankruptcy. In the early 2000s, diversification had seen its finances take such a hit that speculation of hostile takeover was quite real. Tastes for toys are ever changing, competitors constantly innovating, and channels to market shifting, so Lego strategy often has needed to remember its core consumer. Recovery began in 2004 and a return to brand values was boosted by tie-ins to Lego-themed movies and video gaming. In 2017, however, Lego reported its first decline in revenue and operating profits since 2004 and now, under the stewardship of new CEO Niels Christiansen, faces a period of consolidation for a return to stability.

Aside from restructuring the company from within, digital marketing will be important in achieving this. E-commerce, digital technology and growth of social media have changed the ground rules of marketing. Visit the Lego.com website and the home screen offers two choices – for grown-ups to 'explore' and for children to 'play'. Whichever way you go, Lego wants you to do these in the spirit of its company values and mission of education through imagination and problem-solving skills. How is Lego aligning itself with the digital native (those born in the twenty-first century) as well as with their parents and grandparents? Here are a few ways:

▌ licensing future Lego movies, apps and video games to reach movie-goers, gamers and consumers with spin-off toys and special editions

▌ incorporating more technology into its products so that children, or parents, can operate toys via an app, which also provides interactive games

▌ maintaining a social media strategy. Lego has 564 thousand followers on Twitter, and 3.6 million on Instagram, but its main focus is on YouTube, where its channel has over 7 million subscribers

▌ continuing co-creation in new product development with fans on 'Lego ideas' where they work alongside the company's famous design teams.

Digital marketing opens a new resource for the organisation as it researches what its consumers want in the future (the consensus is that this means novelty (will home 3-D printing be next?), where most growth will come from (Asia, mainly) and how it can harness the brand loyalty and enthusiasm of its fans. Ultimately, it may be Lego's family-run ethos and long-term planning horizon (up to 50 years) that will be the key to navigating the uncharted oceans of digital marketing.

DAY BY DAY PRACTICE

If possible, speak to those responsible for, or enthusiastic about, the digital marketing strategy in your organisation. How is it defined? What are their concerns? What is your organisation doing about the use of social media platforms in its marketing and branding?

The product life cycle

A product, according to Philip Kotler, is 'anything that can be offered to a market to satisfy a want or need'.[7] The term includes not just tangible goods but services, too. An experience, a cause, a person or even an idea, all these are potentially viable offerings as long as there is a market for them. Traditionally, the focus in marketing has been on how to present features of an offering in terms of benefits for a customer. Perceptions of benefits and the value they present change over time, something that the product life cycle expresses (see Figure 6.2). Popularity grows, peaks and then eventually wanes. In fact, a product is defined by this time-based phenomenon of shifting tastes and demand.

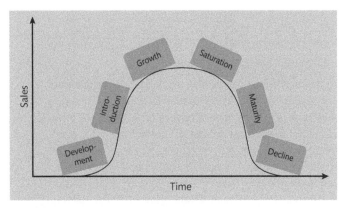

FIGURE 6.2 The product life cycle model

A successful product has phases. From development and introduction to market, to sales growth and then a plateau of maturity, before eventual decline. This is the background to many of the functional areas we looked at in Part 2 (planning for delivery of a good or service, management of cash flows and investment, and proper management of the people involved). For those involved in marketing, this cycle is also a guide for where and what to do tactically and strategically for the replacement or extension of products. Communication around this concept is, therefore, a two-way necessity between all departments in an organisation.

DAY BY DAY PRACTICE

1. Describe the features of one or more of the brands in the organisation you work for (or the branding of your organisation, if this is more appropriate).

2. Select one product or service in your organisation and try to establish in your own mind where on the life cycle model it currently is. What options are there for managing it? Then canvas opinions of others in different functional areas. If appropriate, check this with senior management.

Relationship marketing: customer retention

The scope of modern marketing is being extended through a combination of the internet and the pressure on organisations to grow by maintaining profitable margins. Gaining customers is one thing, but retaining them is now seen as the best route to margin and the best way to do that is through what is known as relationship marketing (RM).

Aside from customer retention, RM has the following characteristics:

▍ Quality is a concern for everyone (highlighted already in Chapter 3 but now driven by feedback from the end user).

▍ Standards of service in points of contact with the customer, measured against expectation and against competitors.

▍ A long-term and personal relationship with the customer, and attempt at alignment with their values.

▍ Measurable returns in terms of net present value (highlighted in Chapter 5) in excess of transactional marketing tactics.

Customer relationship marketing (CRM) is a further refinement of this, often in the form of investment in IT and database management. CRM is supposed to be under the control of general management rather than just a feature of the marketing department. However, the disadvantage of it being under general control is that it tends to monetise the relationship with the customer. Short time horizons in many companies make the customer relationship one of short-term targets in order to achieve returns on any investment. Long-term benefits may be more important but are harder to show on paper. Even when a company is fully committed to CRM, it's not easy to get right. For example, making bold customer care promises that are then not kept is very destructive, and even a genuine wish to engage with the customer can easily be translated into a kind of 'stalking' (e.g. follow-up surveys after every transaction).

Business-to-business marketing (B2B)

Millions of businesses are suppliers to other businesses and, of course, millions more are themselves customers for innumerable products and services from other suppliers. It's likely that many of you reading this book are employed in organisations that rely – in one way or another – on relationships and transactions with other organisations. Business-to-business marketing shares many similarities with business-to-consumer (B2C), but there are some important differences. In B2B:

▌ buyer behaviour is reportedly driven more by logic than by emotion, though values are often key to setting the boundaries for what is and what is not acceptable. B2B may involve a buy decision that involves many individuals (some of whom may even be people with emotions!).

▌ both parties need to pay attention to the value propositions of the other. Aligning yourself to meeting the needs of your customer's customer creates a strong value proposition in its own right.

▌ the cost of a sale is generally much higher than in B2C and so is the complexity of the buyer–seller relationship.

Players in a supply chain tend to be conservative and they prefer more permanent relationships with each other (unless they find reasons not to). For a corporation, relationships with end users are much harder to fix. In contrast, consumers face less risk and have more choice in their purchases and will easily switch, unless they find reasons not to.

Reputation

Reputation is the extent to which an organisation and its products remain consistent over time in the eyes of its stakeholders. A well-accepted definition of corporate reputation comes from US academic Charles Fombrun, who says it is:

> a perceptual representation of a company's past actions and future prospects that describe the firm's overall appeal to all of its key constituents when compared with other leading rivals.[8]

This is broader than brand management. We usually think of this comparison, says Fombrun, in terms of character, emotions, trust and values. The 'substance' or structure of an organisation can and will change; people come and go, products travel through life cycles of growth and decline, and assets accumulate and diminish in value, but reputation is not found in any of these things. Every subject mentioned in *MBA Day by Day* is involved with reputation and, though it holds a special place in strategic marketing, there is a finance, accounting and governance aspect, too. Corporate reputation is not a fixed asset, although many companies have tried to offer a balance sheet valuation of the premium associated with their company reputation. Nor is it always possible to measure the effect of what are usually said to be its main components – credibility, reliability and trustworthiness – on the profit and loss account. Nevertheless, the lure of analysis in management is strong and various devices and models for reputation measurement exist.

Metrics that you might encounter for reporting reputation include:

- opinion polls and market research
- customer satisfaction indices (e.g. net promoter score)
- financial ratios
- internal surveys and statistics (e.g. customer complaints, staff turnover)
- social media reports (e.g. aggregator sites, referrals, hits, tweets, etc.)
- regulatory compliance and quality certification (e.g. ISO).

The reason organisations pay attention to this is simple: there is a correlation between the positive regard perceived by your stakeholders and their willingness to engage in supportive activity with you. In other words, reputation impacts value creation. The risk to an organisation from reputational failure is considered as serious as any other sort of crisis.

DAY BY DAY PRACTICE

1 Who manages the relationships with suppliers to your organisation? If you can, speak with them about how they see the B2B marketing process.

2 What percentage of your organisation's annual turnover is spent on marketing? How would you go about benchmarking this?

Putting it together: a matter of life or death? Marketing is much more important than that

Marketing is tied closely to behaviour because it's what organisations do, as perceived by their customers. Customers care about the 'ends', which are the products they experience but increasingly they care also about the 'means', or the practices used to make and deliver those products. It's easy to see how trust could be built or destroyed by refusal to act ethically and in line with the law or with generally accepted norms. There is plenty of room for grey areas, though. All the 7Ps of marketing have ethical dimensions. For example, where does a company draw the line between a strategy of price differentiation (e.g. creating opportunities for consumers to pay a lower price for the same product) and price discrimination (e.g. some customers having no choice but to pay a different price)?

When you define value exclusively as 'what the customer says it is', you risk taking a viewpoint that ignores other stakeholders, not least the shareholders, founders or owners of the business. Marketing is an exciting, engaging activity, but it is not only tactical. It is the outward, creative expression of strategic creativity. For middle and senior managers, there are still plenty of unanswered questions:

1. **Tactical:** as a function of business, what direction will marketing take next? What innovations to practice will emerge, especially in the digital environment? How can it be managed in such a dynamic environment?

2. **Strategic:** as a business philosophy, is marketing an end or a means to a different end? What will be the role of marketing in the bigger picture of management?

There is little evidence of a major shift in our thinking about marketing. Change seems to be more incremental than revolutionary and, for all its creativity, marketing is following, not leading, the strategic discussion. The critic argues that we are still looking for tactical ways to reinvent the wheel, and strategic ways of making that wheel bigger. But it's still a wheel. It usually takes some kind of trauma to kick-start a period of deep reflection and re-evaluation (similar to an aspect of personal development in Chapter 2).

The term marketing – when used strategically as a whole-business philosophy – includes not only the relationships with customers but that with competitors, too. Without customers you have no business. Without competitors you have no identity. Between these now, as there has always been, is a whole range of influencers (one of the six in the six markets framework). Perhaps it is this rich set of interactions that makes marketing so fluid and unpredictable.

QUESTIONS FOR REFLECTION

1 As a manager, have you ever had to do something you didn't want to do? How were you persuaded? How did you cope?

2 Have you ever made someone at work undertake a task they didn't want to do? How did you persuade them? How did they cope?

Further reading

A classic text: *Marketing Management* by Philip Kotler *et al.* (3rd edition, 2016), Pearson. A hefty book with a hefty price tag, but not much escapes its breadth of content.

Going deeper: *Digital Marketing*, by Dave Chaffey and Fiona Ellis-Chadwick (7th edition, 2019), Pearson.

A Very Short, Fairly Interesting and Reasonably Cheap Book About Studying Marketing by Jim Blythe (2006), Sage Books. A personal and readable account by an experienced author in marketing.

Watch this: 'The most boring ad ever made?' Still one of my favourites – Leica challenges you to watch 45 minutes of careful polishing, and makes its point about the brand: **http://youtu.be/ PpSMW5H7FPQ**.

Notes

1 www.cim.co.uk/files/7ps.pdf.

2 Keith, R.J. (1960) 'The marketing revolution', *Journal of Marketing*, 24(3): 35–8.

3 Porter, M.E. (2004) *Competitive Advantage*, new edition, Free Press.

4 Kotler, P., Keller, K., Brady, M., Goodman, M. and Hansen, T. (2016) *Marketing Management*, 3rd edition, Pearson.

5 McCarthy, J.E. (1960) *Basic Marketing: A Managerial Approach*, Richard D. Irwin.

6 www.hrexaminer.com/the-fair-market-value-of-employees/.

7 Kotler, P. *et al.* (2012) *Marketing Management*, European edition, Pearson, p. 574.

8 Fombrun, C.J. (1996) *Reputation: Realizing Value from the Corporate Image*, Harvard Business School Press.

Strategy
The power of finding clarity in business

All men can see these tactics whereby I conquer, but what none can see is the strategy out of which victory is evolved.

Sun Tzu

In a nutshell

Is a strategy something you have or something that you do? Should a strategy be synonymous with the purpose of business? Or is it just a means to an end? How you connect strategy to other subject areas will depend on how you answer such big questions. Marketing and international business, for example, both have a strategic overlap and any aspect of financial management with capital expenditure or long-term financial interests of the owners is strategic. In fact, you could ask what isn't strategic. No wonder that people love talking and writing about it. In business schools, it sometimes seems that students and faculty rarely talk of anything else.

Make a list of strategic issues that your organisation is facing at the moment. Rank them from most important to least important. What do you think makes these issues strategic? What should you do next? The answer to that last question is what makes strategy such an interesting subject.

Corporate strategy takes the long view and involves a relatively small number of big decisions. Obligated by fiduciary duty to act in the interests of the owners above their own, management are making choices about what markets, with what product or service, and by what means value can best be created. The hard work is only just starting, for it is one thing to set compelling goals in line with the vision of the organisation, and another to follow through. For that, you require the right people, the right structure, enough investment and the correct processes. Business strategy looks at this implementation, often in strategic business units (SBUs). In both cases, strategy means finding and keeping a direction – a sense of purpose – by balancing past, present and future in such a way that the organisation grows.

In this chapter you will:

▌ differentiate between the main approaches to strategy

▌ examine the external and internal strategic environments

▌ define competitive advantage

▌ engage with stakeholders

'Old school' strategy

Strategy, said Peter Drucker, is our answer to the questions: 'What is our business, what should it be, what will it be?'[1] It would be fair to say that Drucker saw strategy as the cement between the building blocks of an organisation.

Invariably, on an MBA, you are told three things about strategy:

1 It is a concept with roots in military campaigns (ancient and modern) and is about victory over defeat. Many people, therefore, see 'winning' in business as

synonymous with strategic thinking. With this comes
the idea that the purpose of strategy is to ensure the
continued survival of the firm, business or organisation.

2 It ensures the long-term viability of an organisation
through sustainable competitive advantage. When the
individual firm is the unit of survival, strategy's function
is to find and then protect from competitors the sources of
value creation. Strategy needs to control the internal and
then exploit external resources of what is defined as its
unique competing space.

3 It is the capstone subject, the one that binds all other
topics in management under one unifying principle. It is
also synonymous with a more sophisticated level of MBA
thinking than the tactical.

The problem of the unique competing space

So, strategy is about winning in the long term and is the
culmination of the journey in management. However,
there are criticisms of this view which we also need to
explore. On an MBA, strategy generally centres itself on
the competitive position of the organisation in what is
sometimes called its unique competing space. This begins
with a search to understand why there is an organisation in
the first place, followed by analysis of the boundary between
purpose and environment (the external and internal bases of
competitiveness).

The problem here is we speak of an ever-changing unique
competing space as if the organisation would still exist
without it. The organisation implies the competing space just
as much as the space implies the organisation. You couldn't
have one without the other. There are two consequences:

1 If strategy wants to be transformational, then analysis
must acknowledge that the unit of survival is never

a single organisation but the organisation plus its
environment. No strategy will be truly transformational
and sustainable otherwise.

2 If strategy equalled only the analysis, your plans would be
left gathering dust on the shelves. Strategy without action
is meaningless. Only when we implement do we find
anything out.

Not for the first time in the book, the crucial link between
strategic sense making or planning and results in the bottom
line is you – the middle manager. Your role is always
strategic.

DAY BY DAY PRACTICE

1 Who decides strategy in your organisation? If possible,
ask what was the organisation's strategy or plan five
years ago. Then ask them what actually happened.

2 What are the basic goals of your organisation? Informally
survey some different levels in your organisation. Does
everyone know what the strategy is?

The structure of strategy

It might surprise you to learn that strategy is a relative
newcomer as a core component of business administration.
During and after the Second World War, interest grew in how
an organisation could sustain itself and, in particular, how
economies could plan to rebuild themselves, and strategy
as its own subject became an explicit part of the MBA
curriculum from the late 1950s onwards, mainly in the USA.
Originally, it was about rational decision making based on
scenario planning, and the use of quantifiable techniques.
This was applied to the organisation in an era of support for

management science, but also one with a new interest in the psychology of human relations, especially in Europe.

On its own a strategy is just an expression of a direction. It needs to be translated from lofty goals and objectives that then must be implemented. The context for strategy is the same as the purpose of a business. Purpose is usually verbalised in mission statements (present-tense expressions of why the organisation exists) and vision statements (future-focused pictures of the goals, ethics, beliefs and values). A good mission statement stands the test of time. Here is how William Macbride Childs, the founder and first vice-chancellor of the university where I work, Reading, expressed the mission of the new institution in 1926[2]:

> Universities are living things: they feel, think and do. They are centres of intelligence; they are concerned with ideas; they have outposts upon the frontiers of knowledge; they sometimes do beautiful and remarkable things; they dream and imagine.
>
> They stand daily in the presence of two of the greatest challenges that can be addressed to Mankind: the challenge to teach, and the challenge to inquire.

What do you make of it? Do you notice evidence of it relating to any of the universal values categories in Chapter 2? How do you think this gets translated into every part of the organisation? Would its abstractions help or hinder the various parts of the organisation discover their own way and "imagine"?

Particular visions, strategies and tactics will come and go as times and leaders change. Powerful ideas are those generate more ideas, so it's a good idea to look around at what other organisations say they are there for, and where they are going.

If strategy deals with competitive threats and evaluates and exploits opportunities, then strategic direction is, in effect, a matter of 'what shall we be competitive in?' This matters because your plans will be judged on whether any changes made can:

▌ increase quality

▌ increase productivity or

▌ free up cash.

No plan survives the first encounter with an event it did not foresee. The unpredictability of the future is the Achilles heel of most corporate strategic planning. This may be one reason why financial markets respond positively to signals of stability and why many senior managers are cautious when protecting the interests of shareholders. Unpredictability means companies identify and minimise risk in many ways (we will look at this in the next chapter), so strategic thinking is a balance between visionary thinking and discounting uncertainty.

Following the energy crises of the 1970s, many organisations started to adopt a way of thinking developed by Shell. Scenario planning accepts that the present is no indicator of the future and that uncertainty about what will happen needs to be part of the process. Future events are seen either as predetermined (i.e. already set in motion) or undetermined (i.e. the consequences of events already set in motion). Scenario planning requires the manager to let go of the logic of current thinking and therefore has a lot to do with awareness and critical thinking about how things work. There are three steps:

1 Identify predetermined elements. What is already happening? What are the current trends that will impact the organisation? How are things connected currently?

2 Ask what sorts of uncertainties these relationships could produce.

3 Develop (up to four) alternative scenarios that reflect the effects of variations in specific, identified uncertainties or boundaries.

Scenario planning is a way to structure thinking. Correctly done (which means 'slowly done'), its strength is that it takes into account the open nature of the environment. It requires a clear vision and attention to detail in planning, but encourages you to scan your surroundings.

An alternative view of strategy is that it must emerge as the organisation grows, from the top down and the bottom up. Most strategists agree that competition is a central characteristic of any free market economy. The orthodox view is that the key to a successful business is the development of a profitable (or sustainable, if not-for-profit) business model that identifies customers, analyses competitive advantage, anticipates competitor actions and looks for novelty and innovation to maintain this advantage. Michael Porter was not the first to write about it, but his book *Competitive Strategy* set the tone for other theorists and practitioners.[3] Porter said that the components of strategic analysis are a firm's:

▌ **external environment:** the opportunities and threats presented by competitors, markets, macroeconomics;

▌ **internal environment:** the strengths and weaknesses inherent in an organisation's resources, skills and microeconomics.

In Porter's models, these are defined and analysed independently, then combined to bring together all the resources required to differentiate yourself in the eyes of your customers. In contrast, Henry Mintzberg sees strategy less as orderly structure and planning and more as 'a pattern in a stream of decisions'.[4] Mintzberg developed a view of strategy as what emerges when your plan meets reality, in the here and now. Crucially, both make middle management the vital link in the value chain because what happens there is what will make the difference for your ability either to achieve or work out a strategy. Porter rather restricts strategy to senior management, who analyse what should be happening. Porter's model also says the firm can and should influence its environment, whereas success in Mintzberg's view comes from a judicious combination of (i) the use of resources at hand and (ii) the speed of innovation.

Internal vs external is a central idea in strategic analysis, as we saw with the SWOT analysis, so let's stick with the approach and look at each in turn.

The external competitive environment

Making sense of the world outside the organisation is one of the main responsibilities of senior management. Failure to do so may result in *strategic drift*, which is where an organisation loses its way over time, often because profits may be good and feedback from existing customers positive. At another level, however, the industry or sector may have moved on and become open to disruption. There are few specific principles to rely on for this external view so the best way to begin is with broad frameworks. The most all-encompassing of these are found in the six categories known as PESTEL:

Political: governments pass laws, set and collect taxes, influence employment policies and intervene in the economy. Where this affects your organisation, you will need to understand how these laws are created and implemented. Transnational groupings such as the EU bring an even wider backdrop of stability (or instability) to this context.

Economic: these are the macro factors that are the boundaries of economic growth, such as interest rates, wage rates, exchange rates, etc. In an interconnected economy, almost every organisation is affected by this aspect.

Social: many cultural norms also influence the business environment, such as population demographics and societal divisions. Public opinion can make or break an organisation's strategy. Shifts in wealth, neglect of human rights, imbalances in gender equality and access to education are all examples of social factors.

Technological: the advances in knowledge brought about by science, the advances in communication enabled by the internet and computational power of computing are all examples of this.

Environmental: this includes concerns over climate crisis, exploration and exploitation of the environment for natural resources, agriculture and the effects of continued urbanisation globally, and the creation and treatment of waste.

Legal: this covers the laws and regulatory environment, including the level of enforcement and exploitation of loopholes in different parts of the world.

PESTEL is used to identify which external factors have the most impact on internal conditions, so a more detailed analysis at the organisational level would follow, based on only those elements that matter. It is a checklist that addresses the question: 'What is the business environment like?' It does not answer the follow-up question: 'Is this a good environment for us?'

For this, we may turn again to Porter. The key model of a firm's competitive environment is his Five Forces model, first presented in a landmark 1979 *Harvard Business Review* article as a reaction to what he saw as the over-simplified format of the SWOT.[5] Five Forces has attracted its critics in recent years but is still widely used. The big idea is that the attractiveness (i.e. profitability) of an industry or sector is the interplay of five factors and you analyse whether the influence on your organisation of each is high, medium or low:

▌ **Rivalry between firms:** the central idea. Competition for market share will be fierce if competitors are well balanced or if consumers can easily switch. If the main players in the market are of similar size and type, or if consumers can easily switch, then rivalry will be high. Intense competition can shape strategy.

▌ **Threat of new entrants:** this will be high if there are few or no barriers to entry to your industry. New rivals can easily force your margins down as you compete for customers strategically. High barriers make this threat less important in your strategy.

▌ **Bargaining power of buyers:** this is high if your customers can put pressure on you, are sensitive to price, or if your structure has high fixed costs and your margins are low. If your customers are large and few, or sensitive to changes in price, then this aspect will have a high importance to your strategy. If switching is expensive for them, then you have more influence over them.

▌ **Threat of substitutes:** this is high if customers can easily (i.e. cheaply) meet a need or a want in another way. This is why Coca-Cola owns so many other ways of satisfying your thirst. If a need can also be met by completely different products or services, then the attractiveness of the whole industry may be in question.

▌ **Bargaining power of suppliers:** this is high if you rely on only certain suppliers, or those suppliers would have a low cost to switch away from you to other customers (the inclusion of suppliers and buyers links to Porter's value and supply chain concepts mentioned earlier).

Porter's model has been 'top of the pops' for a long time and is worth applying because it forces you to ask some good questions about your business model. Its limitation is that it assumes possession of perfect information and that the context is relatively stable. Complexities in the contexts surrounding each of the Five Forces are not reflected in the analysis and there has been little empirical evidence that any industry or sector actually conforms to this model. Nor does it easily explain alliances and cooperative behaviours among players in a market, which are commonplace.

The internal competitive environment

The external approach scans the world for its nature and its opportunities. You start with what you find. The internal approach to strategy starts with what you know you have got and with the things you know you can do best. The resource-based view (RBV) measures your company's competitive advantage in terms of:

▋ **intangible** asset of human capital (***knowledge management***, and the talents, skills and experience of people) and their social capital (the networks that those people have)

▋ **tangible** assets of equipment, machinery, reputation, funding, and so on.

To form an advantage, however, these resources need to be difficult for your competitors to imitate. They must also provide access to important market segments and contribute to the value proposition.

DAY BY DAY PRACTICE

1 What does your organisation have that others near you in your competing space could not easily imitate?

2 What does your closest competitor or comparison organisation have that would be difficult for you to copy?

The internal view is an argument to make strategy based on your core competencies. We looked at competencies for individuals in Chapter 2, but they have been applied easily to organisations as well. C.K. Prahalad and Gary Hamel were the main champions of this 'inside-to-outside' approach in the 1990s.[6] They proposed combining people skills with technology to foresee what value might look like in the future. However, for them the exercise is not just a list of what you're good at, it is more a willingness to view all qualities of the business as fluid, receptive to change and capable of exploiting future opportunities. Examples of companies that have been agile in reinventing themselves include Nokia (rubber to mobile phones), IBM (from adding machines, to mainframes, to clone PCs, to consulting and IT), Netflix (DVD rentals to subscription online streaming and original content) and India's Wipro (vegetable products to IT consulting).

Many organisations with a large enough critical mass can reinvent themselves in subtle ways. Xerox, for instance, now sells more services than copiers, while Netflix recovered from a collapse of sales in rental DVDs to re-emerge as an online giant streaming content, including its own productions. Enron's rise and very public fall was an unethical form of reinvention, an example of the systemic dangers of hubris and unsustainable greed disguised behind a veneer of favourable company HR policies. The economy is clearly an ecosystem where many more companies will fail than survive, even those with (on paper) all the right ingredients.

Assessing competitive advantage

An organisation's competencies are difficult to define, except perhaps in hindsight. Even if strategy fortune-telling were reliable, competencies can walk out of your organisation before the much planned-for opportunity arrives. The future is, by definition, unpredictable and, despite the number of consultants out there, no one has yet written the definitive book of rules on how to maintain a truly sustainable competitive advantage.

I've mentioned competitive advantage several times now. On a good MBA you always define your terms, so what exactly does the phrase mean? First, there can be no advantage without disadvantage, so this is, fundamentally, a comparison against others (a ratio, in fact). Second, organisations need to be viable to sustain themselves, so this must be tied very closely to cash flow where the advantage is achieved, ultimately, through either profit margins or control of costs. Is this what competitive advantage boils down to? It may be a very relevant question to ask. Scottish economist John Kay's 1993 model for distinctive capabilities lists three sources of competitive advantage.[7] Each is quite difficult to achieve and none fits neatly into any formula or recipe:

▍ **Architecture:** the network of relationships and routines that sustains the identity of the organisation over time. This links us to many other themes in *MBA Day by Day*, such as organisational culture and supply chain management. Architecture includes the strategic managing of knowledge and flows of information. Any such aspect you have but that is unavailable to others constitutes a real advantage because it is systemic and hard to imitate.

▍ **Reputation:** the whole point of pursuing quality is to establish in the mind of your customers that it is worthwhile maintaining their relationship with you. Traditionally, this loyalty was seen as important only for products experienced over the long term and used regularly. In the internet age, I would argue that it is important in every case. This relationship between buyer and seller seeks an equitable balance of exchange. Customers must feel they are receiving value and will be happy to pay for this if they are sure they are respected, and buyers must feel they are not being forced to undersell what they do. Reputation involves the delicate give and take of trust ('trust us, we know what we're doing') and, once gained, is the second source of real advantage.

▌ **Innovation:** the third distinctive capability is the most difficult to turn into a competitive advantage. This may be because of the uncertainties of return on future investments (which we looked at in Chapter 5) or because there are few recipes for introducing new offerings ahead of competitors. If you can do this, perhaps through innovative research and development (R&D), it may well give you an edge. Innovation, though, carries risk. Being the first mover in a market is sometimes a critical element for strategy (as in the pharmaceutical sector), but it doesn't always pay off.

Kay's thinking borrowed from game theory, which did not capture the unpredictable nature of open systems such as consumer markets or, more recently, the globalised economy. He has since refined and added to his ideas and suggests that strategic success is often oblique. That is, in an uncertain world we often end up achieving goals through indirect approaches, not direct ones.

DAY BY DAY PRACTICE

1 If you have access to the senior management team in your organisation or business unit, interview them about their opinion of your organisation's source(s) of competitive advantage.

2 What is your own view on this? Be prepared to answer questions they might have for you.

Choices for growth

Sometimes 'do nothing' is a strategic decision, and it may resemble a move back to core strengths or original value proposition. There are, however, plenty of choices on what kinds of strategy you could follow if annual growth is dictated. Strategy guru Igor Ansoff developed a popular matrix[8] to show the choices available, which are between existing or new products or services, and existing or new markets, as in Figure 7.1. These create four growth strategies:

▌ **Market penetration:** finding new customers in your existing market, either by taking share from a competitor, or perhaps by buying up one of your rivals and taking theirs.

▌ **Market development:** introducing successful products to new customers, for example in new locations or territories (e.g. export, licensing, joint venture, etc.) or even through a new segment.

▌ **Product development:** finding new products to sell to a market you are already in. Extending a product line, or adding novelty, is a good sign of a business idea's health.

▌ **Diversification:** moving into both new markets *and* new products at the same time. Diversification can come in two flavours, either via a portfolio of unrelated businesses or of products (perhaps in a holding) or by combining the product and market development strategies above. Companies can outgrow their single original activity and become multi-business organisations or move up and down their supply chain in vertical integration). The underlying principles of diversifying are worth understanding, even if your organisation never gets there because successful companies often grow by buying up single-business firms (like yours?).

FIGURE 7.1 Ansoff matrix

EAC Japan – strategy on tap

The East Asiatic Company (EAC), a subsidiary of Danish company Micro Matic, supplies keg and counter-top beer dispensing equipment to the four major breweries in Japan that control 95 per cent of supply. The Japanese beer market is different from many other countries. In return for exclusivity among the roughly 500,000 small outlets (averaging 1.5 taps per bar), brewers provide a complete system for serving customers beer of the right size and quality.

Securing supply contracts to Japanese companies takes time and is notoriously difficult for foreign companies to achieve. Price counts less than quality, and assurance of quality is developed through relationships of trust. EAC's clients expect to be involved in the development and testing of equipment before rollout, and expect suppliers to respond instantly and fully to research and remedy any issues, no matter how ▶

minor. The European way of working where the product is developed remotely by the supplier and then sold to the client doesn't work in Japan.

All EAC's direct competitors are long-established Japanese firms. As the only international player in the market, the company must take the long-term view. This often means abandoning business strategy principles that would work elsewhere and partnering with all stakeholders, including competitors.

For William Boesen, since 2013 the CEO in Japan, the implicit corporate strategic challenge set by head office is to grow the company's earnings before interest and taxes (EBIT) by 10 per cent year on year. His problem? In their primary business, dispense heads, Micro Matic already has 100 per cent market share. Revenue streams replacing worn-out keg equipment are yet to materialise, so EAC must develop a business strategy for the next three years.

The answer appears to lie with innovation. However, in Japan, new products can take two to three years until invoicing. Direct sales pitches have little effect when customers require thinking time, written business cases, revisions and lengthy trust-building negotiations. EAC's parent also has its own time-consuming R&D and approval processes, checks on ROI, tooling and quality testing. Breweries typically involve many levels of their management at every step to test and gather feedback (from their customers, too) and so need to be 100 per cent sure EAC will be ready to respond to any issues before going ahead.

William therefore maintains a much broader pipeline of ideas than might be the case in Europe or the USA (perhaps only one or two of two dozen will come to fruition). Strong, local competitors and limited internal resources means just going head-to-head to compete for the most lucrative segments (such as beer coolers and fridges) would carry too much risk.

This case shows the difficulty presented to business units or subsidiaries of aligning corporate strategy to business strategy. Both are future focused, and both wish for the organisation to remain viable and grow, but the business level is where change needs to be formed and implemented, and this is very complex. One of the reasons for this is the need to manage various types of stakeholder.

Stakeholder management

Managers must identify important stakeholder groups or representatives when forming and implementing strategy (a stakeholder is any interested person or entity that potentially has something to lose). In large organisations, this process may be quite formal and can produce enough data to test perceptions widely among other non-core audiences. A typology of the important attributes of stakeholders was provided by Ronald Mitchell in 1997 (see Figure 7.2).

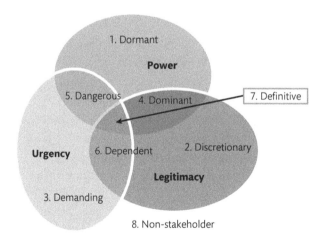

FIGURE 7.2 Mitchell's stakeholder typology
Source: Mitchell, R., Agle, B. and Wood, D. (1997) 'Toward a theory of stakeholder identification and salience: Defining the principle of who and what really counts', *The Academy of Management Review*, 22(4): 853–86. Reproduced with permission of The Academy of Management.

The first step is a judgement of what type of influence a stakeholder might have. In other words, how could it influence your business (positively or negatively) that any given stakeholder:

can choose to do what they want, despite you	*Power*
has a legal or contractual claim with you	*Legitimacy*
demands immediate attention from you	*Urgency*

When these overlap, eight possible categories of stakeholder follow, each with its own action required:

▌ **Dormant:** groups that could impose their will but lack the right and the need to do so. *Action: keep informed.*

▌ **Discretionary:** groups with a legitimate claim but no power to influence anything and no pressing need. *Action: involve only when necessary.*

▌ **Demanding:** those that have an immediate need but neither power nor legitimacy to enforce it. *Action: prioritise other groups first.*

▌ **Dominant:** have both power and legitimate claims on what you do. *Action: keep well informed.*

▌ **Dangerous:** have power and urgency but no right or legitimate say. They expect a say and may resort to disruptive measures to get it. *Action: monitor and keep engaged.*

▌ **Dependent:** lack power but have urgent and legitimate claims. *Action: manage thoughtfully as they can realign with other stakeholder types.*

▌ **Definitive:** possess all three aspects. *Action: full communication.*

▌ **Non-stakeholders:** possess no influence over you.

DAY BY DAY PRACTICE

Look at this list of possible stakeholders: board of directors, management, financers, brokers, shareholders, financial regulators, industry regulators, government or government agencies, consultants, employees, contractors, customers, industry organisations, universities and schools, trade unions, non-profit organisations/charities, the media (you may add others).

Identify at least two of the key stakeholder groups for your organisation that could have strategic importance. Conduct an analysis using the Mitchell typology shown in Figure 7.2.

1 What are some of the strengths and limitations of the methods and models for strategy reviewed in this chapter? How have they helped you understand your organisation?

2 Reflect on your understanding of strategy. In your organisation, how can you become more involved in strategy:

(a) Analysis?

(b) Creation?

(c) Implementation?

Putting it together: the future is unwritten

To paraphrase the Danish philosopher Soren Kierkegaard, strategy must be understood backwards but lived forwards. This is tricky. Strategy is the search for cohesion, so it is interesting how much disagreement there is about its meaning. Perhaps this should not be a surprise. After all, strategy is the subject most associated with sense making and that is not a clear-cut process. In strategy, it is often said that the devil is not in the detail, it's in the implementation. So, how can you transcend the many debates and escape the myriad traps? Here are a few additional questions to prompt your thinking:

1 Is strategy fully defined? The models and theories in this chapter have been based mostly on activities in large corporations, many based in North America. Do these ideas apply to other parts of the world, or equally well to small- and medium-sized companies? What about the public or not-for-profit sectors?

2 Is strategy not the 'grand design' but rather the process of managing tiny feedback loops (known as the iterative process)? Many managers are unhappy with the idea that strategy formulation is a remote process and that planning must precede implementation. Strategy may actually happen at the coal-face.

3 Does strategy have a moral dimension? The standard mantras of competitive advantage and shareholder value have, some would argue, made strategy blind to moral and ethical issues and obsessive about winning.

It is important to raise these questions. International business (the subject of Chapter 9) is influenced by our cultural biases and these, in turn, influence our theories of business and economics. The link between strategy and values has often been overlooked – it requires a long-term view, not a short-term one. In the end, you need to make up your own mind whether strategy is made on the go or brought about by planning. Only you can decide whether it is limited to meeting corporate goals or has a duty to meet social ones as well. We will look at this again in Part 4, under leadership (Chapter 10) and sustainability and change (Chapter 12).

QUESTIONS FOR REFLECTION

1 Do you have any self-limiting beliefs? Try to identify two or three (ask others to tell you if you can't think of any). Write down the assumptions you have made for each belief.

2 Sit still in silence for several minutes, eyes open, focus softened. What do you notice going on around you? Write some notes. Make short spells of stillness a new part of your daily practice.

Further reading

The choice of books on strategy is enormous and it is worth spending some time browsing, so this list is by no means exhaustive:

A classic text:	*The Rise and Fall of Strategic Planning* by Henry Mintzberg (1994), Free Press. The book that challenged many myths in corporate planning.
Going deeper:	*Competitive Strategy: Techniques for Analyzing Industries and Competitors* by Michael E. Porter (2004), Free Press. A clear and concise presentation of Porter's ideas.
	The Outsiders: Eight Unconventional CEOs and Their Radically Rational Blueprint for Success, by William N. Thorndike (2012), Harvard Business Review.
Listen to this:	'The Bottom Line' is a business conversation show on BBC Radio 4 hosted by Evan Davis. More than 260 past episodes are available at: **www.bbc.co.uk/programmes/b006sz6t/episodes/player** or via podcast.

Notes

1 Drucker, P. (1979) *Management*, Pan Books, p. 445.

2 Childs, W M, (1926) The New University Of reading: Some Ideas For Which It Stands, Bradley & sons

3 Porter, M.E. (2004) *Competitive Strategy: Techniques for Analyzing Industries and Competitors*, new edition, Free Press.

4 Mintzberg, H. (1978) 'Patterns in strategy formation', *Management Science*, 24(9): 934–48.

5 Porter, M.E. (1979) 'How competitive forces shape strategy', *Harvard Business Review*, March–April, 57(2): 137–45.

6 Hamel, G. and Prahalad, C.K. (1996) *Competing for the Future*, Harvard Business School Press.

7 Kay, J. (1993) *Foundations of Corporate Success*, Oxford University Press.

8 Ansoff, I. (1957) 'Strategies for Diversification', *Harvard Business Review*, Vol. 35, Issue 5, Sep–Oct 1957, pp. 113–24.

Finance 2: corporate finance and governance
You really should know what your business is worth

> I say, not in a braggadocios way, I've made billions
> and billions of dollars dealing with people all around
> the world.
>
> Donald J. Trump (CNN Republican debate,
> 16 September 2015)

In a nutshell

Corporate finance is part of strategic thinking because
collectively managers must assess, implement and evaluate a
given course of future action in terms of its ability to create or
destroy value. The most common metrics used to measure this
are financial. In Part 2, we looked at finance in terms of reporting
past performance, but this is not the same thing as valuing the
business. A business is worth what it can be expected to do in
the future. Corporate finance is about systematically choosing a
course of action that will create value in the future.

In this chapter you will:

▌ understand how businesses measure value in the future

▌ look at risk and how it may be managed

▌ see how governance structures are set up and work

▌ understand the principles behind, and importance of,
valuation in financial planning

Ensuring the future of the organisation

You don't have to be the manager making the big, strategic decisions for corporate finance to be important. The fact is that you are already involved because those decisions need implementing and you must align what you do to an overall direction. Look back now at the McKinsey 7-S framework. Imagine how each of those elements needs to be aligned for the organisation to maintain balance. In a similar way, knowing more about why your organisation has the capital structure and investments it does makes it easier for you to understand the purpose of your job. Later in your career it could be you deciding which plans to implement, so an understanding of the language and theory of corporate finance will be crucial then.

DAY BY DAY PRACTICE

Arrange to speak with your chief financial officer. Ask them to explain the capital structure of your organisation. What is the balance between equity and debt (gearing)? How is it appropriate to the goals of your organisation?

First we need to restate as plainly as possible what value looks like in finance terms. An organisation with no cash (or access to cash) has no future. It follows that an organisation must be concerned with how it will continue to generate enough cash in the future to fulfil the task of value creation. To do this, senior management has to make three kinds of decision:

1 **Investment:** deciding which projects or assets will produce free cash flows (i.e. investable or distributable returns after adjustment for earnings before taxation) in years to come.

2 **Financial:** deciding where is the best place to source the funding for investment. Is it better to seek new investment from equity or debt, for example?

3 **Dividend:** deciding after other obligations have been paid whether and how cash surpluses should be redistributed among shareholders or reinvested.

Sounds straightforward but, as you might expect, there are some caveats:

▌ In many free-market economies, shareholder wealth is the most important measure of value and generating returns to shareholders is more important than profit. But not all companies, countries or cultures place shareholder value so clearly above the interests of other stakeholders. Interest is growing in alternative models such as production cooperatives, mutual societies, collaborative economies (consumers swapping goods directly with each other) and Islamic finance.

▌ Numbers feel rational, but the quantification of value creation masks exactly how much human judgement and intuition are used in financial planning, which is a lot.

▌ Despite systems of safeguards intended to prevent unethical behaviour, company managers may fail to avoid temptation and put their own interests first. Corporate scandals and greed have been in the news all too often.

Nevertheless, wealth creation remains at the heart of value measurement as it is taught at business school. Wherever you work, fiduciary duty affects what you do. So, let's look at corporate finance decisions through five lenses: governance, valuation, risk management, value and financing. I will focus on what these concepts mean for you as a manager in your day-to-day work rather than what they might mean to an investor (the literature in that area is vast).

Not everything should be summed up in financial terms but valuation is important. It does not require that you know finance inside out; you just need to know enough at least to start to answer the question of the worth of your business. Why? There are lots of reasons. You may be part of an acquisition process, or it may become critical in litigation but, most commonly, it gives you more power for business planning and negotiating external sources of funding. If you don't know what the business you are in is worth, find out.

Governance

We saw in Chapter 1 that representing the interests of the owners or founders is a basic management task. Shareholders are supposed to trust that managers will make decisions without the need for constant monitoring, and managers are not supposed to put their own reward ahead of the interests of the shareholders. This responsibility is called fiduciary duty and is a legal relationship between the principal (owner) and agent (manager).

DAY BY DAY PRACTICE

What is the governance structure of your organisation? Find out what you can about the people who are in governance roles in your organisation.

That relationship, called governance, makes sure that activity carried out by managers is not in conflict with owner interests. In an ideal world – in theory – managers will act only to maximise the interests of owners or shareholders and not to further their own to the detriment of shareholders. Agency theory states that this needs to be governed to make sure that managers don't put their own wealth first. It tries to mitigate this risk by offering senior managers good incentives, often with performance-based inducements, such as bonuses or shares, to fulfil their fiduciary duty and create value. You can see the grey area here as to how far this is a matter of ethics.

It will help to understand the differences between management and governance:

▌ Responsibilities of management:

– Make day-to-day decisions to execute a strategy.

– 'Do things right'.

– Align their actions with the boundaries set by the governing body.

▌ Responsibilities of governance:

– Oversee the whole organisation and its structures, functions and traditions.

– 'Do the right things'.

– Make sure that objectives are met in an effective and transparent way.

– Hold accountability to stakeholders and the wider community.

Boards are appointed by shareholders to undertake this setting of direction and upholding of values and to monitor and check the work of management. They are not involved in the day-to-day running of the business.

CASE STUDY

Theranos

The story of US biotech start-up Theranos is a great case study in entrepreneurship and leadership gone horribly wrong. While study of the character, motivation and conduct of its founder, Elizabeth Holmes, can teach us much,[1] the corporate governance angle – and what it says about the ▶

relationship between founders, investors and regulation – is just as worthy of note.

With no technical or business know-how, Holmes raised $700 million to set up Theranos in 2003. Theranos was to develop and market a revolutionary blood-test system that could run a whole series of diagnostic tests using just a few drops of blood drawn from the finger, without the need for the more intrusive needle in a vein. In a $70 billion market, anyone promising to shorten clinical testing reliably would not only have the ear of the industry, they'd stand to make billions doing so.

Modelling herself on Steve Jobs and Theranos on Apple, right from the start Holmes sold her technology as revolutionary. Everyone wanted to believe her. Obtaining faster and cheaper test results would not only bring massive savings for drug companies and health professionals, patients would suffer less. But although a software start-up can afford to over-state its case and launch with a prototype, a medical company cannot. Holmes got herself into ever-growing traps of her own promises for the technology and wildly ambitious revenue and profit forecasts.

When the company failed to develop a technology that actually worked, Holmes and her COO built a secretive and toxic company culture. Holmes had a self-confidence that seemed to charm the powerful. Almost no one ever challenged what she said; the company always seemed to have the figures. Its market valuation reflected the extent to which investors wanted to buy in to the promises and the cause. At its peak in 2015, Theranos became one of the best-known 'unicorns', valued at $9 billion and its founder a celebrity and role model.

Over time, Holmes cultivated her network of wealthy and influential contacts and protected herself from any criticism through the country's most expensive law firm. In terms of governance, three things stand out:

1 As CEO, Holmes recruited former Secretary of State George Schultz to the board in 2011 and used this to

invite a long list of ex-diplomats and military leaders, including retired general James Mattis, Henry Kissinger and leading attorney David Boise. None had any expertise in bio-tech businesses. In fact Holmes had engineered her shareholding so that the board could not out-vote her and even those board members with business experience seem to have accepted that Theranos did not bother with fiduciary oversight or basic checks as to whether the technology worked.

2 Doing little or no due diligence, the senior management of major retailers such as Safeway and Walgreens contracted to pour money and resources into the Theranos project, not stopping even when deadlines were missed or their own experts warned them of irregularities.

3 Between 2009 and 2016, Holmes and her COO consistently prevented Theranos from coming under the scrutiny of federal agencies such as the FDA, even cheating regulatory and licensing inspections when they occurred. Agencies did not follow up until after the stories broke in the press.

In 2004 Theranos was valued at $30 million. By 2010, after several rounds of fundraising, this stood at $1 billion. In 2014, it had a $9 billion valuation, following investment of $400 million. However, Theranos had fraudulently overstated its revenues and by the end of 2018 the company's valuation was virtually zero. Its investors had lost an estimated $600 million.

Theranos was a private company and, though most agree that she started with good intentions, Elizabeth Holmes created a vicious and secretive cycle of deception and corporate intimidation that became too big to admit. Just before the story of what was really happening was broken by *The Wall Street Journal* in 2018, Theranos was on the brink of launching in stores and clinics across the USA, a step that could have had life-changing (or life-ending) consequences for patients receiving faulty treatment and diagnoses. The lesson is not merely that Holmes was flawed or dishonest, but that those around her charged with oversight did not challenge or impose the governance that would have exposed Theranos sooner. Everyone wanted her story to be true.

Valuation

It is a board's responsibility to create value as a return on money invested by shareholders. Therefore, they need to understand not just the performance of the business but also how much it is worth – its valuation. They will be the ones who make decisions about buying or selling parts of the business (or acquiring others) so it's vital for them to know what the return is, or will be, as generated by a particular investment. Governance addresses risk (and therefore financial risk) as well as valuation. Management and governance need to coordinate for a business to work well.

Senior management is expected to act to maximise shareholder value and minimise risks found in long-term financial planning. Shareholder value is measured using discounted cash flows (DCF), which allows the organisation to address two questions:

1. Will a given future strategy create value for owners/ shareholders?
2. Which future strategy is better than continuing the current one?

Because of inflation, the value of money will decrease over time unless invested. Fiduciary duty means that management must look for, and then be able to justify and evaluate, the best future plan to create wealth. You may have many possible courses of action available to you, so you need a way to compare like with like. The most common way to do this is by a net present value (NPV) calculation, which is the total present worth of a series of future cash flows that has been discounted at a specified rate.

In finance terms, value is created when companies invest at returns that exceed the opportunity cost of capital (OCC) and this is the minimum expectation for any project in its terminal value at the end of the planning period. OCC is a key concept in corporate finance because the money working in one place is missing the 'opportunity' of working somewhere else, and it establishes the measure of performance of an investment in a commercial organisation. The time during which economic return exceeds the hurdle rate (for example, the OCC) is known as the competitive advantage period (CAP). Beyond CAP, the advantage diminishes as returns are eroded to a point where no additional value is being produced. Context means that what is long-term in one industry may be short-term in another, and different parts of different businesses assess things in different ways. Critically, in all cases the past is no guarantee of the future. A planning period will end with a hypothetical point at which you expect your competition to catch up, so to continue to generate value there must then be further investment, and the cycle goes on.

While these principles are known to all players, there is enormous scope for qualitative judgement (and misjudgement) and no amount of number crunching will replace business acumen and experience. Here is where corporate finance meets the many internal and external forms of analysis featured in earlier chapters.

Value has been a recurring theme in *MBA Day by Day*. The importance of value creation is one of the few things that all management experts agree on. The trouble is that there are so many ways to define and measure it. In a publicly traded company such as Apple, for instance, value is undoubtedly measured by the economic return on investment for stockholders. In health service provision, by contrast, value may be the achievement of target improvements in public health. In a family firm, it could be ensuring the next generation has a livelihood.

We tend to monetise it but value looks different wherever you go. If you don't know how it is defined where you work, find out. If no one in your organisation knows, then either you're working in the wrong company or there is a fantastic opportunity for you to lead a transformation.

Remember, when it comes to what things are worth, time is the measure of all things. US investor Warren Buffett, whose company Berkshire Hathaway is ranked by *Fortune* as the 10th largest in the world and consistently outperforms the market (and who famously suggested that while price is what you pay, value is what you get), is a firm believer in the unexciting but critical skill of business valuation. Equally, you may also want to bear in mind that worth and value are not necessarily the same thing. US sociologist William Bruce Cameron put it this way:

> Not everything that can be counted counts, and not everything that counts can be counted.[2]

DAY BY DAY PRACTICE

1 How aligned to future value creation is your organisation's business model? Who in your organisation has the information to answer this question?

2 What is long-term in your industry or sector? How are long-term investments identified in your organisation?

Calculating a discount rate

The valuation of debt covers borrowings, although here, as with equity, there is complexity and volatility (think about the jungle of traded derivative instruments or the background to the US subprime mortgage collapse in 2007) but since prices for most sources of debt are determined by open-market supply and demand, a market rate is available to determine OCC. The initial basis for that rate is the interest earned on government bonds because they deliver a (virtually) risk-free return.

Any uncertainty about the future represents risk, so adjustments for this will also be built into the calculation of a discount rate. There are three broad categories of metrics:

▌ **Free cash flow:** 'free' because it can be distributed to shareholders, cash is discounted over a known period at the appropriate cost of capital. The time in which any returns are in excess of this capital cost is known as the competitive advantage period.

▌ **Economic profit:** measured by, for example, EVA (Chapter 5) or market value added (MVA).

▌ **Cash flow ROI:** a modified internal rate of return (IRR) calculation using cash flows to assess whether investments exceed or fall below the cost of capital.

Risk management

Higher risk suggests higher return, which in most for-profit companies is an attractive proposition. It also has a downside, of course, if the venture fails to produce returns. The future value of risk is, therefore, reflected in calculations of the cost of capital. Financial economists distinguish between two types of risk:

1 **Unsystemic**, which is inherently present in a particular industry, sector, company or even in a narrow set of stocks.

2 **Systemic** (aggregate), which is the instability inherent in the market as a whole. Volatility is a systemic risk: the amount by which returns on an asset may vary over time. The more it varies and the more difficult this variation is to predict, the lower the value of the asset in the present time. The measurement of an asset's systemic volatility is a comparison of asset return to market return and this is known as the beta (i.e. how much it moved, or didn't move, with the market in the past). Interest rates, economic cycles and day-trading are all sources of systemic risk on stock markets.

As nervous entrepreneurs pitching unrealistic valuations on the popular TV show *Dragons' Den* often find to their cost, the value of a company is tied to future cash flows. Every business is different, but management must take into account all the risk factors appropriate to its sector, size and life-cycle maturity, as well as the whole host of internal and external concerns that we looked at in earlier chapters.

Investment decisions: SVA

Shareholder value analysis (SVA) is what corporate finance has substituted for traditional business measurements in many parts of the world. Shareholders' capital is supposed to earn a higher return than by investing in other assets with the same amount of risk. If a company sees equity returns higher than equity costs, value is created. When that value is known, the organisation can act on this to improve its performance, as well as work out how successful past projects have been. Shareholder value can be determined by discounting the expected cash flows to the present at the weighted average cost of capital. So far, we have looked at finance only from the perspective of for-profit enterprises, which aim at generating free cash flows for their owners or shareholders.

The investment side of corporate finance covers stocks, shares and financial markets for managing investments and risk and would take more than a section in this book to cover. Since our focus is on the types of decisions middle and senior management need to make internally, knowing how a particular investment or project is attractive in value terms is more important.

The attractiveness of a proposed course of future strategic action is determined by its discounted cash flows. This brings us back to the capital structure of an organisation and to the weighted average cost of capital (WACC), which is a calculation of opportunity costs averaged across the capital structure of the organisation, reflecting the risks associated with debt and equity. WACC is a calculation of the percentage and cost of debt plus the percentage and cost of equity. The function of a corporate WACC is as a discount rate. In other words, the level of return on capital needed for an investment must be better than employing that debt or equity elsewhere. This approach is part of value-based management (VBM).

VBM, though, is under severe scrutiny following the near collapse of the economic system in many of the world's mature economies. When all that matters is that every decision is evaluated in terms of the effect on shareholder wealth, the dynamic between the owners and the managers acting on their behalf is thrown into sharp contrast.

It is worth noting here that things are a little different in the case of not-for-profits (e.g. community groups, charitable trusts, non-governmental organisations (NGOs), social enterprises), where the aim is not to accrue wealth but to serve the aims of members by maximising the marginal effect of operations on the capital donated. Value here means human well-being. Can this still be measured by cash flows? Not exactly, but the idea of the time value of money is still useful to evaluate competing options for long- or short-term welfare benefits.

In many countries, the funding of the health care sector (especially if it is a public service funded by the state) is a significant – and complex – subset of valuation because it is not always obvious how to put a monetary value on health benefits. Should only the costs of interventions be compared, or rather costs versus benefits?

Small and medium-sized enterprises (SMEs) cannot generate the kind of data for the capital assets pricing model (CAPM) or for beta calculations, so the quickest solution is to replace many of the variable elements of SVA with market-driven substitutes (for example, by identifying and using the betas of traded companies with similar debt/equity ratios and similar economic influences). Value in SMEs is a broader concept than in traded companies, so the market value often is seen as being the price the owners would get if they were to sell the company. That may be arrived at by:

1 valuing the firm's assets, which usually indicates the business is not viable and needs to be broken up

2 comparing what similar companies are worth (rather like valuing your house by looking at house prices around you)

3 expected future income. This last one is the most common, but may take into account all sorts of other factors, such as competitive position, industry life cycle, type of customer base, scalability of the business, and so on.

DAY BY DAY PRACTICE

1 How good do you think the discounted cash flow method is for valuing a not-for-profit?

2 What role do you think the personality of the owners plays in valuing an SME?

Financial planning

Financial planning combines strategic decision making with the capital structure of the whole organisation into the future. Chapter 5 established where this process begins – with awareness of the current situation using financial statements and ratios. There is a lot of wriggle room for interpretation in statistics and ratios, so when it comes to planning rather than formulaic answers, you want this information to provide good, common-sense questions about the long term. When you get down to it, planning for the long term (i.e. beyond the coming 12 months) involves the following:

▌ **Preparing for contingencies:** 'what ifs' are the difference between simple forecasting and strategic planning for various scenarios (Chapter 7).

▌ **Weighing up all the angles:** a strategic direction may not always be set with only one thing in mind. A move in a new direction may have non-financial imperatives, such as laying the groundwork now in something that enables other, future steps.

▌ **Bringing it all together:** properly done and clearly communicated, long-term plans can unify by providing a perspective for all parts of an organisation and by linking the consequences of managerial decisions at all levels.

We've seen that the main sources of funding for future growth and investment are equity and debt.

Equity is money invested in the business by shareholders, usually in the form of shares. Additional money may be raised by the sale of new shares and, usually, this is in the expectation that funds will go towards non-current assets. Equity attracts returns in the future through payments of dividends from excess residual funds, but equity holders carry more risk (they are not first in line for repayment) so will expect a higher rate of return, which they will also discount to present value to make sure it is invested well. Shareholders are closer to the running of a business than financial institutions, so this can bring additional pressure to bear on senior management to aim for short-term gains.

Debt, meanwhile, is money lent to the business by investors or financial institutions without the expectation of a say in the aims or purpose of the business. Debt offers a fixed claim to interest payments and may offer a slightly lower cost of capital than equity because the lender knows that they have preferred status for repayment. Finding the right balance of long-term funding is not easy. Many companies try to match long-term assets to long-term borrowings or equity, but prefer to maintain liquidity in working capital financed from inventories or short-term securities.

Capital budgeting is the annual listing of major investment projects and these are expenditures that will, presumably, bring some future benefit if properly implemented. All such decisions must consider:

▌ the current and future composition of the organisation's capital structure

▌ whether the size and balance of current asset structure is right for the expected returns, and how that structure should change in the future

▌ the size of funding needed to finance future asset structure.

The ratios mentioned in Chapter 5 can be useful in addressing some of these issues because they are all in relationship with the capital structure. What you, as a general manager, are looking for is:

1 a way of explaining present and past performance, and

2 assessment of risk and return in future activity.

This leads to the further question of the best sources of capital because, as we have seen above, equity and debt carry different costs and can have implications for valuation. All of these options will produce changes to the capital structure, which is why it is important to find out from your finance staff what is appropriate for your organisation.

Organisations may change their capital structure in more radical ways. Here are just a few:

- **Merger or acquisition:** legally, a merger is the creation of a third entity from the coming together of two others and an acquisition is the new ownership of one organisation by another. However, the distinction is often blurred, as what occurs in law can be very different from what is experienced by all those concerned.

- **Leveraged buyout (LBO):** a (private) takeover funded mostly with debt from institutional investors, usually as a prelude to the rapid sale or radical reorganisation of assets. Collateral comes from the expected cash flows or existing assets of the target.

- **Spin-off:** this is when a potentially profitable part of a going concern is sold off as a separate business with, initially, identical ownership structure (and perhaps management team as well) in both old and new.

- **Carve-off/divestment:** a privatisation would be an example of this in the public sector but in the private sector usually it can indicate the removal by sale of unwanted assets. Reasons for doing this may vary but often include a wish to return to a particular core competence or activity, indication of under-performance of a part of a portfolio, fundraising, or as a requirement imposed by regulatory bodies.

- **Bankruptcy:** a legal status that indicates the inability (of a person) to pay one's creditors. However, when applied to the 'corporate person', bankruptcy may indicate a more subtle and controlled (protected) relationship with creditors, whereby commercial activity may continue. This form of arrangement may vary from one country to another.

DAY BY DAY PRACTICE

1 Take another look at what your organisation does. How do you see it in light of what has been discussed in Part 3 so far? What has changed in your perception?

2 What are the new questions you have about your own role? Make some notes.

Putting it together: governance in an age of market failure

Corporate governance is what ties together the various strands in this chapter. Governance and agency theory refer to the structures in place in an organisation to represent and protect the interests of owners and shareholders. If the agent possesses asymmetrical information of a kind that may damage or destroy shareholder value, it could lead to dilemmas, such as:

▌ **moral hazard:** behaviour that takes advantage of asymmetric information after a transaction

▌ **conflict of interest:** behaviour of an individual due to multiple interests, at least one of which is in direct opposition to the interests of the principal (owner).

In some countries, governance of larger, publicly traded companies is legislated for and codified. Structures that organisations put in place to mitigate the risks of governance failures include managerial incentive schemes, takeovers, board of directors, pressure from institutional investors, product market competition and organisational structure, all of which can be thought of as constraints that affect the process through which risk and returns are distributed.

> **QUESTIONS FOR REFLECTION**
>
> **1** Reflect on the best and worst pieces of financial advice that you have received in your life, or your best and worst experiences with money. What advice would you pass on to others?
>
> **2** Do you have a long-term financial plan? Do you want to retire in the traditional sense? What do you see yourself doing at that age?

Further reading

A classic text:
: *The Wealth of Nations* by Adam Smith (1982), Penguin Classics. The book that brought us 'the invisible hand' and 'the division of labour', Smith's 200-year-old classic was one of the first explorations of the market economy.

Going deeper:
: *Bad Blood: Secrets and Lies in a Silicon Valley Startup* (2018), by John Carreyrou, Picador. A riveting and forensic account of the rise and fall of Theranos.

: *Economics: The User's Guide* by Ha-Joon Chang (2014), Pelican books. An accessible and thorough introduction to macroeconomic principles and theory.

Watch this:
: 'Sir Adrian Cadbury reflects on properly constituted audit committees and boardroom self-evaluation.' An interview with the chair of the Cadbury Committee on corporate governance, part of the wide range of additional business materials freely available online: **https://youtu.be/ZfC7ykLKy4M**.

Notes

1 You are strongly encouraged to read John Carreyrou's meticulous exposé of the Theranos story, *Bad Blood* (see Further reading in this chapter).

2 Cameron, W. B. (1963) *Informal Sociology: a Casual Introduction to Sociological Thinking* (Random House studies in sociology)

Global and international business
The grass is always greener?

> 'Curiouser and curiouser!' cried Alice ... 'now I'm
> opening out like the largest telescope that ever was!
> Good-bye feet!' (for when she looked down at her feet,
> they seemed to be almost out of sight, they were getting
> so far off).
>
> Lewis Carrol, *Alice in Wonderland* (1865)

In a nutshell

When your daily work is dominated by tactical thinking,
globalisation and international business can seem like remote
concerns. Don't be deceived, though. You are already part of
the global economy, even if you work in a small organisation
with no apparent multinational involvement.

This chapter looks at two things. First, macroeconomics
and the terms used in policy making for nations, groups of
nations and institutions that regulate international trade.
Then, a survey of multinational enterprises (MNEs), which
are corporations with headquarters in one country and
networks of subsidiary, affiliate or acquired companies that
are hosted in others. Companies may choose to grow outside
their domestic markets for several reasons. They may be
opening whole new markets with new products, or adding to

existing customers in new places. They may be looking for economies of scale, new capital or new skills. Perhaps it's to protect themselves from takeover at home. We will look at these in context.

In this chapter you will:

▌ define key macroeconomic terms and theories

▌ look at the nature of the international business environment

▌ understand how the global market forces and firms shape strategic thinking

▌ see how organisations measure international competitive advantage and choose channels for growth

How beautiful is big?

Take a look at Table 9.1 showing Fortune's top 20 global companies ranked by 2017 turnover. Do you recognise all the names? If not, you may want to look them up. Once you have found out who they all are, what strikes you about the list?

You may have noticed the number of energy companies represented (7 of the top 10). Not long ago, this top 20 would have been a balance of oil and gas producers, manufacturers and financial institutions. That's one aspect, and here is another: the 2005 Fortune 500 Global list contained a total of 16 Chinese companies; in the list published in 2018, it contained 120. The balance of the world economy is shifting – new markets are not just opening up, they represent whole new ways of doing business. At the same time, note that just 10 countries account for nearly all the companies in the top 500. Globalisation also consolidates.

TABLE 9.1 Fortune's 2018 top 20 global companies ranked by turnover

Rank	Name	Revenues ($ m)	Profit ($ m)	Sector
1	Wal-Mart Stores	500,334	9,862	Retailing
2	State Grid	348,903	9,533	Energy
3	Sinopec Group	326,953	1,538	Energy
4	China National Petroleum	326,008	(-690,500)	Energy
5	Royal Dutch Shell	311,870	12,997	Energy
6	Toyota Motor	265,172	22,510	Motor vehicles
7	Volkswagen	260,028	13.107	Motor vehicles
8	BP	244,582	3,389	Energy
9	Exxon Mobile	244,363	19,710	Energy
10	Berkshire Hathaway	242,137	44,940	Financials
11	Apple	229,234	48,351	Technology
12	Samsung Electronics	211,940	36,575	Technology
13	McKesson	208,357	60,381	Wholesalers
14	Glencore	205.476	5,770	Energy, mining
15	United Health Group	201,159	10,558	Health Care
16	Daimler	185,235	11,864	Motor vehicles
17	CVS Health	184,765	6,622	Health Care
18	Amazon.com	177,866	3,033	Technology/ retail
19	EXOR Group	161,677	1,569	Financials
20	AT & T	160,546	29,450	Telecom- munications

Source: Fortune Global 500, 2018[1]

In number and in magnitude, MNEs have ballooned in the last 60 years thanks to regional waves of privatisation, economic liberalisation and market deregulation. In fact, MNEs now account for the majority of the economic activity in the world and embody, in practice, much of what is taught on an MBA. They embody power, too, driving foreign direct investment and supporting first and second tiers of supplier companies. Multinationals have clout, so when international or very powerful companies fail, the fallout can be spectacular. The actions of rogue individuals can sometimes severely damage or even ruin a going concern, as happened after alleged sexual misconduct by Hollywood producer Harvey Weinstein was made public. When issues arise from a systemic mismanagement or deceit, the consequences for the business and its environment can be severe. Enron's collapse in 2001, BP's 2010 Deepwater Horizon drilling platform explosion and ensuing oil spill, the role and conduct of social media platform Facebook in the 2016 US Presidential election, the falsification of data around emissions from diesel engines that has affected some of the world's largest car manufacturers, all these hint at very serious governance issues that can affect public trust and confidence in business as a whole.

Corporate failures are happening all the time, of course. Most new ventures fail and many businesses go through a life cycle that results in natural maturity and decline (or acquisition). Despite the enormous number of companies in the world, mostly we examine and base our management theories on either the big (too big to fail?) survivor stories or the spectacular failure ones. Little attention is paid to what lies in the middle. Even less attention is paid to the dynamics of the ecology of the total population of organisations. Failure is so important in business – and every manager has a relationship with it. Corporate failure, even among multinational giants, can have positive repercussions. When Nokia, at one time the world's largest supplier of mobile phone handsets, was surpassed by its competitors and went into decline, the company cut its global workforce by 24,000 and sold its mobile phone business to Microsoft in a deal worth more than $7 billion. The aftermath of this turmoil and headcount reduction in Nokia's home country of Finland has been a resurgence of high-tech company start-ups using that talent.

DAY BY DAY PRACTICE

All companies need to experience growth when they start and we have become used to the idea that one purpose of a business is to get bigger.

1 For you, is growth a question of maxima (constantly getting larger) or optima (reaching an ideal size)?

2 Does your organisation have an ideal size, or should it keep growing?

The question posed for managers by globalisation is to understand the role and purpose of business as it relates to the macroeconomic environment. Later in this chapter, I want to consider how firms act in the international business environment, but first let's take a look at some macro-level economic principles.

Macroeconomics

Macroeconomics is the study of the economy as a whole. It is the basis for long-term policies and interventions that promote development (growth) and limit the impact of economic cycles. Like all aspects of economics, it is concerned with scarcity of resources, but on a much wider scale than the micro world of the organisation.

Several hundred years ago, wealth creation meant the wealth of nations rather than shareholders. The nation-state

preceded the corporation as the unit of analysis. The idea
was first developed by Adam Smith in 1776, and still has an
attraction for some economists who study the comparative
advantage of one country over another in the production
and trade of various types of goods or commodities. The
metric (and rule of thumb) most often used for the economic
activity of a country is its gross domestic product (GDP),
the total output of goods and services for a given territory
and time. Simplified, GDP looks at household spending,
investment and consumer confidence, government spending,
and volumes of exports/imports. Regional aggregates of GDP
are telling. According to World Bank data,[2] in 2017, the
combined GDP of the G7[3] economies was $36,720 trillion
(45 per cent of the world total of just over $80 trillion). By
comparison, the same figure for the whole of sub-Saharan
Africa (49 countries) was $1,649 trillion (2 per cent of total).

Macroeconomists are as interested in supply and demand,
pricing and the supply of money as microeconomists, but
at an aggregated level. Money supply and demand/supply
of goods are the basic ingredients for inflation and are all
connected in complex flows of rise and fall in outputs, prices
and international trade.

National competitiveness and economic growth

The modern corporation did not begin to emerge until
the end of the nineteenth century. Historically, large and
powerful trading corporations, such as the British East India
Company, grew from the patronage of state, monarchy and
colonial military ambition. Following the Englightenment
in the seventeenth and eighteenth centuries, amid powerful
advancements in science, production and economics in Europe,
following the Enlightenment, East India trading companies
were set up to exploit Austrian, Dutch, Danish, French,
Portuguese and Swedish national ambitions of trade with Asia.

The World Trade Organization (WTO) was set up in 1995 and coordinates trade agreements and negotiations among 159 member countries. It has promoted the removal of many barriers to trade and (controlled) freedom of movement of capital and labour has superseded the protectionist outlook that dominated before the 1970s. In fact, few countries can now afford to act in their own interests without being part of international (regional) trade agreements such as NAFTA (North American Free Trade Association), the EU (European Union) or ASEAN (Association of Southeast Asian Nations).[4] Economically, everyone is connected. In 2001, former Goldman Sachs chairman Jim O'Neill coined the acronym BRIC to highlight the importance of four emerging economies (Brazil, Russia, India and China) to the global economy in the coming 50 years. Recently, he has come up with MINT, four countries (Mexico, Indonesia, Nigeria and Turkey) identified as the next centres of economic growth. Transnational organisations such as the IMF or the World Bank act as checks and balances on the flow and supply of money:

- **Fiscal policy (demand side):** the tactical or strategic use by governments of revenues and taxes in public expenditure to influence key macroeconomic factors, such as employment, investment and industrial output.

- **Monetary policy (supply side):** the use (most typically) by central banks of interest rates to influence inflation, with the aim of maintaining economic stability in the medium and long term.

- **Trade and exchange rate policy:** increasingly being coordinated by members of the trading blocs, though severely under scrutiny following the subprime mortgage collapse in the USA, the euro crisis in the EU and a decade of stagnation in Japan.

It's worth restating that most of the world's economies are based on capitalism, albeit in several forms. China, with a communist political system, has been fairly clear about the role of market capital in the economy since the 1990s, with results that none can ignore.

The international business environment

Senior management needs to look at the macro factors in their environment that can influence their primary goals, or that might advantage their competitors. In the previous chapter, we looked at this through the lens of a PESTEL, first introduced in Chapter 7. This is usually applied from the point of view of a single organisation, as it looks outwards but, for the student of international business, a PESTEL may be applied to the whole industry or sector, as in the example in Figure 9.1 for the banking industry. Which factor(s) do you think are the most important for the various stakeholders in the banking industry?

DAY BY DAY PRACTICE

1 Construct an industry PESTEL analysis of the widest possible environment as it affects your industry.

2 Which elements stand out to you as being more important? What should all organisations in your industry be paying most attention to?

There are three sets of questions to ask about international business:

1 Why do businesses move outside their original national borders? What is the motivation?

2 How do they enable themselves to do this? What channels are available?

3 Which is the right channel to become international? Why do different firms choose different ways?

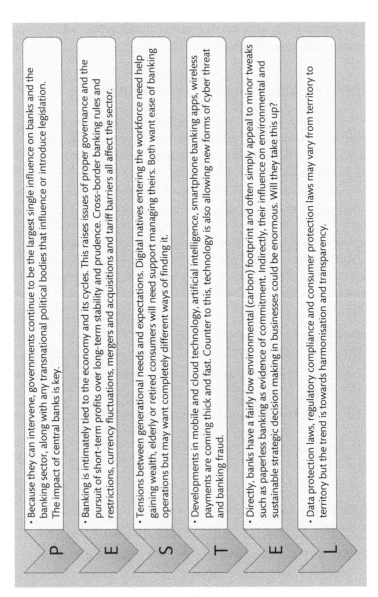

P • Because they can intervene, governments continue to be the largest single influence on banks and the banking sector, along with any transnational political bodies that influence or introduce legislation. The impact of central banks is key.

E • Banking is intimately tied to the economy and its cycles. This raises issues of proper governance and the pursuit of short-term profits over long-term stability and prudence. Cross-border banking rules and restrictions, currency fluctuations, mergers and acquisitions and tariff barriers all affect the sector.

S • Tensions between generational needs and expectations. Digital natives entering the workforce need help gaining wealth, elderly or retired consumers will need support managing theirs. Both want ease of banking operations but may want completely different ways of finding it.

T • Developments in mobile and cloud technology, artificial intelligence, smartphone banking apps, wireless payments are coming thick and fast. Counter to this, technology is also allowing new forms of cyber threat and banking fraud.

E • Directly, banks have a fairly low environmental (carbon) footprint and often simply appeal to minor tweaks such as paperless banking as evidence of commitment. Indirectly, their influence on environmental and sustainable strategic decision making in businesses could be enormous. Will they take this up?

L • Data protection laws, regulatory compliance and consumer protection laws may vary from territory to territory but the trend is towards harmonisation and transparency.

FIGURE 9.1 PESTEL analysis of the banking industry

It is estimated that the world's largest 500 MNEs now account for about 80 per cent of the world's foreign direct investment (FDI) and that 75 per cent of these companies are headquartered somewhere in the triad of the USA, the EU or Japan.[5] Why might this be so? Michael Porter looks to answer this question using an extension of his thinking on industry competitive advantage. The Porter diamond is the result of research into what appeared to be the reasons for success among companies in clusters of industry types and locations.

Six aspects form an overall framework for analysis. Four are country-specific, potential determinants of advantage and they interact and influence each other. There are also two external variables of **government** and **chance** that can act on the four:

- **Factor conditions:** include those human, physical and capital resources available as supply of inputs in a location.
- **Demand conditions:** include market size, segmentation and access to consumers.
- **Related/supporting industries:** mainly seen in terms of partners in the supply chain of inputs.
- **Structure of firms and rivalry:** Porter believed that the presence of intense rivalry was the most important aspect driving the others.

The main criticism of Porter's diamond is that it analyses a situation using only the conditions in the host country as if it were a closed system. This is not exactly realistic, as national economic systems are often closely interdependent with each other. American academic Alan Rugman doubled the diamond in order to include determinants from both home and host country, in the original study it was Canada and the USA. He suggested that the firm should consider both as one if it wants a strong basis for building a regional or even a global business.[6] This is sensible, and often borne out in reality, as firms assemble assets and assess the various determinants in Porter's model in contexts that are regional. Within the European Union, for instance, the interplay of strategic decision making with country-specific factors in neighboring states has been a major driver of economic success within the bloc. More significantly, strategic oversight of any clusters of industrial, service or support activities is what gives flagship multinational organisations such a much strong reach globally.[6]

Globalisation is sometimes confused with international business but it is a bit more than that. It is the concept of a completely integrated, homogeneous and open worldwide economic system in which inequalities are gradually removed by economic development. Not only is that going to be very hard to measure, even as an ideal it is far from current reality because it is evident that large parts of the world, and most notably Africa, are comparatively poor. Globalisation is a study (by optimists or by pessimists) of barriers, tariffs and segmentation, and of the exploitation of economic or political inequalities for economic gain, and is therefore an aspect we will consider in Chapter 12.

For now, on closer inspection the majority of the world's MNEs may be said to have regional strategies, not truly global ones.

The macroeconomic approach

FDI was once seen as the rational search by a company for a superior return on its capital employed by making an investment overseas. In practice, it's often a lot more than capital that is invested, and in a lot more than just equity.

Investment involves expanding a portfolio of business interests, blurring the boundaries between domestic and international:

▌ Supply-side reasons may explain MNEs moving location to where it costs less to produce.

▌ Equally, a demand-side wish to exploit untapped markets may be the reason.

▌ An MNE can take advantage of lower material costs in one place while out-supplying local competitors in their own market somewhere else.

▌ The removal of, or special exemption from, tariffs and trade barriers may be a key driver as large firms then move in.

▌ MNEs are often able to access much cheaper financing than local firms and their capital structure allows low-cost debt in strong currencies to trade in markets with weak ones. Because capital markets and national economies are cyclical and volatile, this may explain short-term cycles of takeovers.

CASE STUDY

International business strategies

International business is a bread and butter topic for many of the world's largest companies, and their major suppliers. While small- and medium-size companies (SMEs) risk much to fulfil their hopes and dreams of moving beyond their domestic roots, MNEs tend to hedge and protect themselves well to withstand periods of ambiguity, and rarely suffer life-threatening consequences from their investment or expansion decisions. Their experience and their wealth can mean they will act swiftly, decisively and with agility to take advantage of market conditions, as well as mitigate against losses, disposals or write-downs. When it comes to investment and expansion internationally, tried and trusted formulae tend to be the norm, though there are exceptions. For example, Kaman. ▶

Kaman – a $1.8 billion global company with only one JV

Founded in 1945, the Kaman Corporation is a $1.8 billion, publicly traded company with main divisions in aerospace and industrial distribution that cover a host of civil and military engineering products, systems and businesses in over 50 countries. Kaman's strategy has long been through targeted acquisition and complete control rather than from organic growth or strategic partnerships. In 2013, Kaman Aerospace Group entered in to a joint venture (JV) agreement with Indian start-up Kineco to manufacture advanced composite structures for the aerospace & defence industry. Kaman prefers to own its businesses and broadcasts its acquisition strategy on its website. The JV (Kineco Kaman Composites – India) is unique in Kaman as their only such venture. The equity position is 51 per cent Indian and 49 per cent Kaman, and the split is regulated by Indian foreign investment policy. According to Kaman's CEO Neal Keating, the new venture was brought about to reduce customer costs, and has been a success, with revenue growth of 20 per cent or greater year on year, and employees now numbering 180. Kaman's original decision in 2012 to pursue the JV was intended to offer customers a lower-cost labour solution and target the growing offset obligations of major aerospace OEMs who are selling military systems to India. Offset rules are extensive, but there is a requirement of 'indigenisation', that is, a 'buy Indian' requirement for 30 per cent or greater of the contract value.

Consolidated company accounts reflect bigger trends and are valuable for business students to analyse broadly where an industry or company stands. We can sometimes overlook how even these larger corporations are susceptible to the same localised investment risks and dramas as SMEs. For example, Kaman's fourth quarter results for 2018 revealed a strong headline set of figures for growth and sales over the same period in the previous year, despite a $5.7m one-off loss incurred on the sale of what had been a $5m green-field investment in a Tooling plant in Burnley, Lancashire in 2014.

Macroeconomic theory suggests that MNEs can also be explained by comparative advantage, that is, countries exporting and importing to capitalise on relative strengths and weaknesses in their available national resources or markets. For this reason, MNEs go where there is an efficient supply (for that country) of resource or labour.

The microeconomic approach

This tries to explain the MNE more in terms of the thinking that goes on inside the organisation. Senior management teams are:

▌ duty-bound to reinvest for growth wherever there is a better net return to be found, and they will physically follow where their market is growing. What starts out as a success in one market then moves to export to another, which in turn leads to competition and the need to adopt a suitable strategy for internationalisation

▌ culturally better informed by their experience of foreign markets in general and this encourages MNEs to spread

▌ trained to look for opportunities where a monopolistic or oligopolistic competitive advantage can be gained. This follows the idea that perfect competition cannot really ever exist – there will (even only for historical reasons) always be differentiation and inequalities in markets. The organisation that is best attuned to these is the one best placed to grow and expand, taking advantage of the economies of scale that being an MNE can provide.

Economies of scale become standardisation, which in turn allows localisation of a central idea with adaptation (at a lower cost than a local provider can match) of goods and services in new markets. In short, managers use their knowledge of business administration principles to create value by choosing the lowest-cost location for any activity and grow by direct ownership of these assets (as long as the benefits outweigh the costs). Here we begin to understand the activities of MNEs as just an extension of the efficient management of resources outlined in all the chapters of Part 2.

Managing the two levels

This tension between seeing things from either a national or an organisational perspective is expressed in terms of one framework, the CSA–FSA matrix. CSA stands for country-specific advantages, which are those strengths such as geographic location, government policies, natural resources, human resources or levels of technology that nation-states may be said to possess or have access to. FSA refers to firm-specific advantages, or factors traditionally counted as strengths within a company or organisation (many of which we have been looking at in earlier chapters). Occasionally, the boundaries between the two become confused. The interests of Chinese technology giant Huawei, for example, may represent something at both levels of structure and strategy.

John Dunning, a leading authority on the theory of the multinational firm, summed up many of these aspects into three types of advantages that determine why and how firms go international – ownership, location or internalisation (OLI).[7] Ownership advantages are basically the same as the FSA features, while location advantages map closely to CSA. Internalisation advantages reflect how an organisation chooses to act on those perceived sets of advantages. Which routes or channels a firm should use to internationalise was, for Dunning, a question of best net return once all risk factors have been taken into account (as we saw in Chapter 8). Just because you can, it doesn't mean you have to – expansion should not be a matter simply of a rush into new markets with capital investment unless alternatives can be shown to be less effective.

Putting it together: four routes to internationalisation

There are four main routes that an organisation can use to move its scope beyond the borders of its home country:

- **Export:** usually the first channel to try, this form of trade is 'as old as the hills'. Exporting represents the lowest risk but is susceptible to government tariff policies, the power that any intermediaries might exert and exchange rate risk as currencies move in relation to each other.

- **Licence:** permission or rights given to a partner in the host country, in return for a fee, to trade in the (intellectual) property of the home company. The licensee often carries the majority of the costs and risk, but may also take a larger proportion of the margin than a distributor for an export.

- **Contractual agreements/joint venture (JV):** a JV may be the most sensible step into new markets in territories that are developing or emerging, or towards the sharing of know-how in preparation for closer cooperation. Finding a good match with a JV partner in terms of size, ambition and culture is really important. High levels of patience and trust are required. Many JVs fail because the time horizons set for them are too short to build a relationship.

▌ **Foreign direct investment:** ownership of the entity and its assets in the host country, with consequent transfer and flow of home capital, know-how and (at least to begin with) management personnel. FDI, which globally has been falling in recent years, may be via acquisition or green-field investment and gives the highest level of control – at the expense of agility or flexibility in exit. FDI is the costliest strategy, so any such transaction costs associated with the extra need to be less than the net advantage gained.

In reality, firms may employ more than one route or strategy, and the intricacies of international trade tariffs and tax regulation mean things are rarely as clear-cut as the theory would suggest.

QUESTIONS FOR REFLECTION

The term 'worldview' describes your fundamental orientation, embedded in collective culture, shared language and individual experience, covering all your basic beliefs.

1 What is your worldview? Are you a global corporate citizen?

2 Think about your current work colleagues. What worldviews and perspectives exist among them? Do you understand those viewpoints? Can you hold your view and their views at the same time?

Further reading

A classic text: *International Business,* by Simon
                         Collinson, Rajneesh Narula and Alan
                         Rugman (7th edition, 2016), Pearson.

Going deeper: *Globalization and Its Discontents
                         Revisited: Anti-globalization in the
                         Era of Trump* by Joseph Stiglitz (2017),

Penguin. Nobel laureate Stiglitz offers
a critique of the mismanagement of
globalisation that has prevented it
being a force for good.

Watch this: 'Actually, the world isn't flat.' The
2012 TED talk by Pankaj Ghemawat
that cautions us to be more
precise when we conjecture about
globalisation: **www.ted.com/talks/pankaj_
ghemawat_actually_the_world_isn_t_flat.**

Notes

1 Fortune.com/global500/att/.
2 http://wdi.worldbank.org/table/4.2.
3 Canada, France, USA, Italy, Japan, UK and Germany.
4 The Brexit vote in the UK and the election of Donald Trump to President
in the USA have been part of a reaction and a questioning of this among
economists and politicians in a number of countries.
5 http://unctad.org/en/Pages/DIAE/World%20Investment%20Report/World_
Investment_Report.aspx.
6 Collinson, C, Narula, R & Rugman, A M (2017) *International Business*, 7th ed.
Harlow, UK: Pearson.
7 Dunning, J.H. (1977) 'Trade, location of economic activity and the MNE: A
search for an eclectic approach', in Ohlin, B. Hesselborn, P. and Magnus, P.
(eds), *The International Allocation of Economic Activity*, Macmillan.

part

Visionary MBA thinking: how to embrace change

Visionary n. ['vɪʃnrɪ]: thinking about or planning with imagination or wisdom.

T he final part of *MBA Day by Day* is about demonstration of mastery of choice in management practice. Tactical thinking is learned on the job, in trial and error as well as by apprenticeship. It helps managers align the parts of the organisation they are responsible for with the strategic goals set from above. Sometimes, as happened early in the story of Swedish furniture company IKEA, a tactical action (removing the legs of tables to fit them into a delivery truck) leads to a strategy, but usually tactical thinking comes later and remains uncritical of the assumptions behind strategic thinking.

Strategic thinking is endlessly analysed and studied at business school. It is how managers establish a direction and set of plans for the future, and it drives the majority of the theories and models of management. A good MBA will bring you this far. A great one will require you to go one step further. Problems in management do not come in neat boxes marked 'people', 'marketing' or 'finance', and so on. The segmentation of business administration into subjects, silos or departments may be convenient, but it is also arbitrary. How you bring all this together is by visionary thinking.

Visionary thinking needs your judgement and wisdom if you are going to get that strategic thinking right. When you think about it, being visionary means being ahead of your time, seeing something that may not be clear to others until much later. You may start as a lone voice, and you may face opposition, barriers and obstacles. To begin only with an idea requires resilience, humility and intelligence on your part. 'Success' in leadership is always fleeting because the world is always changing and moving on, and you may also need to redefine what success is.

Visionary thinking needs *practical skills* for systematically solving a problem, a *moral* or *ethical compass*, or principles for navigating the power relations and inequalities or imbalances in human relations, and a *holistic understanding* of the relationship between a business and its environment.

Every chapter in this part of the book is about change. The goal of stability (endurance at the level of survival) depends on retaining an ability to change (adaptation to circumstances).

The purpose of this is to release you from **lineal** thinking in problem solving and to reach maturity in how you manage the dilemmas and uncertainties inherent in all management contexts. The four chapters in this part of the book are:

- leadership
- entrepreneurship
- sustainability
- 'just start walking'.

This is integral to changing your thinking and developing your self-awareness, the two lasting benefits of doing an MBA mentioned in Chapter 1.

Leadership
The mindset of purpose, vision and change

> Talent hits a target no one else can hit; genius hits a
> target no one else can see.'
>
> Arthur Schopenhauer

In a nutshell

Of all the subjects in *MBA Day by Day*, leadership holds
the greatest promise for both personal learning and
organisational development. Our culture has given us many
iconic ideas, theories and images around leadership, yet
we have found it very difficult to agree on one definition.
This chapter will consider the key concepts and theories
of leadership and how they are applied to change in
organisations.

Skills as a leader are perhaps the greatest expectation by
employers of people who have an MBA, yet an MBA is
never a guarantee that its holder is going to be effective in a
leadership role. Leadership is as much about followership
and followers as it is about leaders. Because of its
transformational potential, I want you to think critically
about leadership and this means deliberately questioning
some of the assumptions behind the beliefs that you and
others hold.

In this chapter you will:

▌ understand the different ways of defining leadership

▌ establish a difference between managing and leading

▌ review the main theories and models of leadership

▌ contrast the traditional view of the leader with a systemic view of leadership

Why we talk about leadership

It's a truism that the need for good leadership has never been greater, and no one can deny that our interest in leadership is at an all-time high. There are three reasons why:

1 **It is *really* relevant now.** Our general belief is that we live in increasingly complex and challenging times. In the next 10, 20 or 30 years, sustainability, economic emergence of the developing world, population growth, poverty and environmental concerns, geo-politics and demands on scarce resources – as well as ideological diversity in management itself – will all require a response.

2 **There is demand.** Organisations in those emerging economies will be switching from manufacturing to knowledge. Value is now less anchored to tangible assets. As companies grow by acquisition and merger, they will look for figureheads with vision, energy and ideas who can influence other people's behaviours.

3 **There is also supply.** Organisations need leadership and being placed in the role of leader brings that individual influence and authority, which is a popular idea in our culture. Leadership is a social norm and acceptable goal for all aspiring managers. The cult of the leader can have a toxic side, too: leaders can be seen as both the solution and the problem. But perhaps this means we should not look for leadership only in the personality of the leader.

Are you a manager or a leader?

Is there a difference? It doesn't take long for this question to come up at business school and people have enjoyed historically debating it in the spirit of the age. Our views change with the times but it might be fair to say that managers try to organise what already exists in the best way possible, which means also making plans to keep doing that into the future. Management is about consistency of the present in the face of what is to come. Leadership, on the other hand, actively steers towards a future that would *not* just happen by management alone. Leading is a conscious, deliberate movement from the known to the unexplored and untested, usually undertaken where there is higher risk and initial opposition. What justifies this may be greater rewards than would otherwise come, or a response to a threat or opportunity that is outside the scope of the organisation's current capacity or competence.

Broadly, there are four major perspectives on the source of leadership:

▌ **From authority and hierarchy:** this views leadership as granted to those naturally best suited to it. This may be down to certain traits or innate qualities, or simply the product of position in society. Being born into or being naturally suited for leadership is, perhaps, the oldest view – and it explains why leadership training was once an elite and exclusive type of education (very different from our modern approach).

▌ **From competencies and skills that are learned:** this sees leadership as a profession, where people can and need to be prepared (trained up) to lead others whenever called upon to do so. Different personalities may develop different leadership styles, but it is definitely a learnable skill, even a vocation.

▌ **From its activities, tasks and practice:** leadership pops up to deal with whatever needs to be done when there is a collective need to overcome a challenge, problem or crisis. In other words, it is the need that conjures the leader, not the other way around. There is still often a belief that 'the right person for the task' is important, so a link to competencies is maintained.

▌ **From the relationship we all have with the system:** complexity may look messy but from a holistic view studying leaders in isolation is half-baked; a bit like studying a marriage only by observing one person. Without followers, there are no leaders and vice versa; the concept of leadership makes no sense except in context. Systems thinking suggests that leadership is defined in wider systems.

The first three are covered by the conventional views of leadership in management today, especially in large organisations, and they have in common that leadership can be understood by studying what leaders do or who leaders are. In other words, you need to understand the individual. Only the fourth, the systemic view, does not isolate the leader from the context of leadership.

In summary, some theories focus on the skill, tactics and characteristics of people, while others try to understand what leadership is by seeing how it emerges from a context or situation. In both cases, however, the contrast between managing and leading is the next thing to consider.

DAY BY DAY PRACTICE

1 Before you read the next section, consider your thoughts on the question 'Am I a manager or a leader?'

2 Which of the four schools of thought, above, on the nature of leadership makes most sense to you?

Management vs leadership

What people study on an MBA are the tools, techniques and theories for analysing, planning and controlling. The task is for an organisation to perform effectively and efficiently and meet or exceed its goals. This feels solid; it sounds like management. At the same time, MBAs are told that they are also in preparation for leadership in times of change and uncertainty, where flexibility, creativity and 'out-of-the-box' thinking are important. This feels less concrete. Leadership is much harder to grasp because it concerns things that do not yet exist. Both management and leadership deal with values as well as value, both address purpose as well as process, and each can claim it aims for achievement as well as attainment. Both happen in the present moment.

My take on this is that the crucial difference comes from leadership being about a future state. Management as a mindset struggles with the future and acts to minimise unpredictability. Leadership as a mindset thrives on that.

Leadership is found in many parts of life, which is one of the reasons it is difficult to define. In business, the scope of leadership is anything and everything that is a challenge to the stability or future of the organisation. Managers who are leaders are also still managers. Unless you own the company, your management task is first and foremost to protect the interests of the owners, founders or shareholders. A tension comes because leadership is a kind of exploration and this involves risk. Leaders have to be risk takers, of course, but there are limits because the new course must still perform the managerial goal of creating value.

DAY BY DAY PRACTICE

1. Talk to some of your colleagues. Do they consider themselves to be managers or leaders? The more people you can talk to, the better equipped you will be to form your own definition.

2. What is the main leadership task in your organisation? How is this currently measured?

The development of models of leadership

Earlier in the chapter, I told you there were four major perspectives on leadership. There are also many models and theories. In the next section, I'd like to give you an example of the range available. It's not a complete list, of course, but all are well-established and, as you read, you might want to reflect on each from your own experience, or from examples of leadership you are familiar with.

Leadership as authority, hierarchy and innate quality

Trait theory says leaders are leaders because they possess a set of innate qualities and characteristics. 'Leaders' are born with these traits; they cannot be developed. This theory dates back to Thomas Carlyle's 'Great Man' theory in the mid-1800s. History, it was said, was the story of the biography of great men (women were almost entirely excluded). This now seems dated, but echoes of trait theory live on in the growing interest in charismatic leadership and in tests such as the 'Big Five' personality questionnaire, which assumes that innate, psychological qualities play a part in our ability to undertake leadership roles.

Trait theory relied largely on **inductive** (see **Inference**) observation; it saw successful examples and then drew wider generalisations and predictions based on those. Transactional models of leadership, where leadership is based on hierarchical positions of power over subordinates, also rely on this logic. Over time, the theories and models have been adjusted, but this view of leadership can become a self-fulfilling concept.

Leadership as learned competencies and skills

If Drucker is the first voice in management writing, veteran scholar Warren Bennis can claim the same for leadership studies. In 1985, with Burt Nanus, he published *Leaders*, a book that has set the tone for the subject ever since.[1] Bennis was influenced by the hardships of the Great Depression but also by the series of iconic leaders in the decades following. This formative experience comes across in his four requirements for leadership:

1. An adaptive capacity for being resilient, creative and aware of opportunities.
2. A capacity to engage followers and align them around a common goal.
3. The undertaking of a life-long process of self-awareness.
4. A moral compass or set of principles and convictions.

On top of the subject-specific knowledge each sector or business requires, Bennis is a firm believer that leadership has a moral shape and that it can be learned.

Leadership style is all about behaviours rather than personal characteristics. Leadership is what leaders are able to do and how the leader copes with the balance between concern for the task and concern for people. This model is very popular because it fits easily into existing ideas about the role of management and so is used extensively in organisations.

The two sets of concerns translate nicely onto a leadership grid with five styles, developed in the 1960s by Robert Blake and Jane Mouton and shown in Figure 10.1.

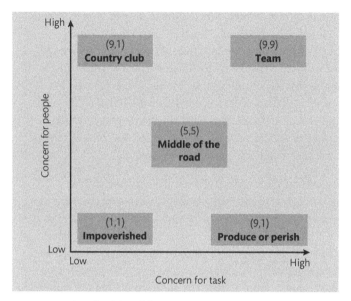

FIGURE 10.1 Leadership grid
Source: Adapted from Blake, R. and Mouton, J. (1985) *The Managerial Grid III: The Key to Leadership Excellence*, Gulf Publishing Co. Reproduced with permission.

The grid began life describing managerial work, so its claim to say something about leadership leaves open the question whether there is any difference between the two.

Leadership as activities, tasks and practices

The idea of leadership as a process and not a list of attributes, skills or traits moves the topic closer to a more contextual (and strategic) view. A process suggests that leadership occupies the space between leaders and followers. Leadership can then be more distributed and may appear at many levels. The leader's role is still multifaceted but is more subtle than earlier models because followers are now just as important to the concept of leadership.

Situational leadership starts from the idea that different situations call for different kinds of leadership. It is an extension of the leadership style model because it says that a leader adapts their style and develops their skills in order to meet the varied needs in each situation. Situational leadership begins to recognise that leaders interact with followers (in fact, there is no leader until there is at least one follower). Based on the work of Paul Hersey and Ken Blanchard, the model puts forward the idea of a connection between the leader and the readiness of the follower that establishes leadership as relational.

There are four leadership styles, each associated with a different context in the management of people, processes and projects. The first of these is *directing* – appropriate when your followers have high commitment but low competence. This may be typical of the start of employment or kick-off of a new project; sometimes people just need to be shown or told what to do. A second, more supportive, style – coaching – is suitable when your followers already have some experience of what they are doing but still need or look for direction, though in this context coaching often looks a lot like training. As your staff gain in confidence, they can take more responsibility for themselves and their tasks. The third leadership style is when you remain high in terms of being *supportive* but more hands-off when it comes to you giving direction. Typically, you will intervene either when asked to, or through your own questions. Lastly, at its most developed level, situational leadership requires low levels of support and direction, and you are *delegating*, trusting that your staff will flag up any issues when they come across them. The implicit idea is that leadership is being transferred downward over time.

Situational leadership is popular in management development because it fits with conventional views of organisations as hierarchical but complex, and also with the widely held opinion that leaders should change to meet changing needs of subordinates. It relies on the leader, however, to make the running. They need to read the situation (and are therefore separate from it) and know exactly the levels of competence and commitment among those lower down in the organisation. Two theories of leadership attend to relationships between people in an organisation. The first is Leader-Member Exchange theory (LMX), the other Transformational Leadership theory.

Popular in North America, *LMX* observes patterns of in-group and out-group formation found in many companies. This is an informal system of leaders relying on certain people over others. It develops parallel to the formal organisation structures of job functions as they are on paper. LMX says the reality is that leaders will attract or find certain people whom they trust to get things done, and they should work with these in-groups to use talents well. This can be effective, but the theory doesn't lay out how this should happen, and it also has been accused of being unfair to the out-group.

The theory behind *Transformational Leadership*, as developed by Bernard Bass, combines humanistic concerns for employee well-being and empowerment with metrics around the delivery of change. The leader acts to influence others to achieve collective and individual transformation. They do this by using their own personality, morals and skills across four 'I's:

Idealised Influence	being a role model
Inspirational Motivation	leading to trust and admiration and the wish to work harder
Individualised Consideration	genuine concern for others
Intellectual Stimulation	challenging others

The catch in these theories is that the leader sits above others and imposes control from on high. This brings us to a set of theories that frame leadership a little differently.

Leadership as humility and service

Lao Tzu, founder of Taoism in China, managed to capture a very modern take on leadership many centuries before it emerged in our post-industrial society:

> A leader is best when people barely know he exists, not so good when people obey and acclaim him, worse when they despise him. But of a good leader who talks little when his work is done, his aim fulfilled, they will say: We did it ourselves.[2]

Several recent and influential theories have said much the same. *Level 5 leadership* arises from one of the most robust studies of leadership, conducted by Jim Collins, whose book *Good to Great* ought to be on every manager's reading list.[3] After a longitudinal study of nearly 1,500 companies, what Collins found surprised him. Only 11 companies made the transition from strong performance to consistent outperformance of others in their sector. In every case where this was achieved, the person in charge was not the outgoing, high-profile and larger-than-life character that usually appears as a role model in the media. Such stars may be effective in the short term, but they tend to bring division and personal ego to the organisation. Collins noted that great leaders, in commerce at least, began by surrounding themselves with the right team and then credited those people for any success. Collins also found that great leaders are strong-willed professionally while humble personally. He called these people 'Level 5' leaders. They have egos but their energy is focused on service of the organisation and not on praise for themselves (you might think back to the Erikson life cycle in Part 1 and the topic of generativity). Collins found that such leaders had often undergone a personal trauma in which they had learned this life lesson.

Good to great companies:

▌ confront current reality head-on with the belief that they will survive

▌ take their time in getting things done – they keep steady and do not swing wildly from one change programme or restructuring to the next

▌ keep their business model simple – you find what your passion is, do the one thing you are best at, engage the right people in the process. This is sometimes known as the 'hedgehog concept', innovating only in line with what you already do well (i.e. the hedgehog knows one thing, the fox many)

▌ are highly disciplined in rejecting hierarchies and bureaucracy while highly focused on promoting activity, new ideas and entrepreneurship.

Servant leadership is a strongly ethical extension of the logic above. The idea – put followers first, and empower them – was developed by retired AT&T executive Robert Greenleaf in the 1970s. Servant leadership is part of a participative style of management, where the manager or leader is effective without resorting to hierarchy or authoritative power. A servant leader, according to Larry Spears, influences in 10 ways:[4]

▌ **Listening:** being receptive to the group and helping to clarify what they want.

▌ **Empathy:** accepting others and seeing things through their eyes.

▌ **Healing:** an appreciation of the natural ability of others to be whole.

▌ **Awareness:** starting with self-awareness.

▌ **Persuasion:** building agreement through sound argument, not coercion.

▌ **Conceptualisation:** finding and nurturing vision in self and others.

▌ **Foresight:** intuitively understanding past lessons, present realities and the likely outcome of a decision for the future.

▌ **Stewardship:** remembering to be in service of the needs of the system.

▌ **Commitment to the growth of people:** personal, professional and spiritual.

▌ **Building community:** the pursuit of societal justice, well-being and progress and concern for the underprivileged.

A servant organisation puts its people before profits. This contrasts with the conventional view of organisations as places where personal development is a nice-to-have and not a must-have. However, there is some confusion over whether servant leadership is prescriptive (this is how to do it) or descriptive (this is how people have done it). In addition, the link between the goals of the organisation and the goal of societal change is often difficult to identify.

DAY BY DAY PRACTICE

1 Choose a specific example of leading or leadership from your own experience. Then look at it again through the lens of one of the leadership models presented above.

2 Which framework did you choose? Why?

Again, all these theories of leadership locate it in the role of a person who is a 'leader'. We may never shake off the habit of defining leadership in terms of the role played in it by an identifiable leader, but the concept 'leadership' is more complex than this.

Where is the study of leadership going next? *Authentic leadership* (AL), the newest member of the theory family, might be showing us the way. US author and academic Bill George popularised AL as an extension to the transformational leader's strong sense of purpose and values, building relationships of trust with others, and being sensitive to their needs. What's new is the self-discipline to act *always* in line with one's values and principles. Being authentic means knowing what is going on inside your own mind and aligning this with your interaction with others, but it is also about how others respond to you. AL develops over your lifetime, and can be affected by trigger events. Without a strong ethical element, it risks becoming power abuse, so the authentic leader applies four principles:

1 *Self-awareness* through continuous reflection.

2 *An internalised moral perspective* whereby decisions are not reached from outside pressure.

3 *Balanced processing* of all points of view.

4 *Relational transparency* by being open and honest with others about what they think and feel.

Authentic leadership is popular and has many promising things to offer individuals who need guidance on how to develop in leadership positions. It, too, though, is all about 'the leader'.

CASE STUDY

Leadership flows in from context?

We love stories about leaders, but is the narrative of the leader the same thing as leadership? We all seem able to recognise what leadership is, yet explaining it beyond the personality or behaviours of the leader is tricky. Leadership is too important to place on the shoulders of individuals, so how else could we look at this? Traditionally, we think of leadership inserted into a situation (or not) by the leader. The leader first, leadership follows.

We could try flipping this conventional wisdom around by saying that, when the conditions are right, context responds by activating the space for leadership. ▶

We might say that when the follower is ready, the leader appears, and the question is only whether they are effective or not. Humans are an interactive, purposive species, and we have survived in part because societies will tend toward norms that look after the health and well-being of the group and its members. Whenever there is a threat (from minor or existential), certain behaviours emerge or are activated in response.

Let's briefly look at three scenarios – individual, organisational and societal.

1. You are driving along and a road accident occurs suddenly right ahead of you. You are not involved or injured, but your way is blocked. You are first on the scene, alongside three or four other people. In what ways is leadership called for here?

2. A large company in the middle of merger talks finds out that computer hackers have gained access to its customer database and have compromised large amounts of data over a period of six months. Is there leadership required? How?

3. A city has grown from a population of 6 million in 2006 to approximately 17 million by 2018. It is forecast to grow to 37 million by 2050 and to 88 million by 2100. Is this a leadership question?[5]

Each has its own time horizon, but what they all have in common is change with potentially serious consequences if nothing is done. The need to respond creates a vacuum and leadership fills this as the situation unfolds. Every scenario also gives individual agent the potential to step up, take on roles to bring about or enable a change, and this is what most leadership theory looks at. But individual decisions interlock with the decisions and actions of others, so leadership might best be understood as a web of distributed leader stories.

Looked at this way, leadership ties together everything in this book.

Leadership as a systemic phenomenon

A systems view challenges many assumptions underpinning the last 60 years of theory in leadership development. An organisation is a system, and every system implies a dynamic trade-off between the internal and the external environment (markets) such that it can continue to exist as a distinct entity. Businesses and organisations, markets and economic conditions, societies and civilisations are all forms of open systems. To some extent, they are unpredictable and complex and, therefore, you cannot hope to understand them simply by analysis of their parts.

Systemic leadership explains how a leader is only one part of the sense making of a wider context. Complexity theory says that an organisation is not a closed system with fixed variables and linear processes but rather it is an open, or complex adaptive system (CAS). Complexity leadership provides a model for leadership as an emergent property distributed in the interactions between the inside and the outside of an organisation, some of which will be random or chance. Given enough variety in a business system, says this view, leadership is bound to emerge. Researchers Benyamin Lichtenstein and Donde Plowman identified four conditions for this:[6]

1. **A dis-equilibrium state:** something happens that is out of the ordinary and this initiates a real imbalance in the system. This sort of crisis is sometimes known as 'the edge of chaos'.

2. **Amplifying actions:** when a system is not in equilibrium, small actions or events can create differences that jump across in a non-linear way and produce unexpected changes in other parts. These are positive feedback loops (positive here signals an exponential increase in a response in the system). If enough of these occur, a threshold of change eventually will be crossed by the system.

3. **Self-organisation:** under these changing conditions, the system will either collapse or it will reorganise itself into

a new order or new state. The system is, in some way, 'learning'. The process of change here is highly creative (i.e. it is volatile and disruptive) and eventually negative feedback loops (negative means it is self-sustaining) are needed to check the positive ones.

4 **Stabilising feedback:** positive feedback cycles in a system eventually will be dampened by negative ones to some kind of stabilisation. These negative loops are imposed from a higher-level system (e.g. the market). The organisation adjusts to the new situation.

In each phase, leaders may choose their own actions and behaviours, which are part of the system, too. A leader may embrace and even exaggerate uncertainty when faced with it and they may act to support people in the organisation as they try to make sense of change. The leader may even act to calm things down when the system is ready to return to a steady state. The main difference between complexity leadership and other theories of leadership is that explanation of what happens is found in the way that a system works, not in the way a personality is measured.

DAY BY DAY PRACTICE

Watch the 2016 TEDx talk titled 'Great leadership comes down to only two rules', by Peter Anderton, **https://www .youtube.com/watch?v=oDsMlmfLjd4**, which tracks the question of leadership over two millennia and comes up with a couple of very simple conclusions. As you watch, make some notes.

Is he right?

Discuss this, if you can, with colleagues or friends.

Because our current economic model is materially successful, but as yet still unsustainable, future leadership may need to bring about a systemic change. This will mean local, regional and global changes in public policy to influence consumer behaviour and different reward systems for founders and investors of businesses. Above all, it calls for a new phase in leadership theory and this is perhaps the most exciting – as well as the most challenging – aspect of where we are now. Complexity leadership is not a recipe of what to do. Sooner or later, though, the question of what to do will come up, because every theory of leadership deals in change.

QUESTIONS FOR REFLECTION

1 Do leaders create leadership-shaped solutions to fit problem-shaped holes, or do problems create leader-shaped solutions to fit leadership-shaped holes?

2 Is leadership about improvisation or rehearsal?

Leadership and change management

Traditionally, one name dominates the subject of change as it intersects with conventional ideas of leadership: John Kotter. Leadership isn't about dreams and visions, it's about dealing with the fact, says Kotter, that at least 70 per cent of change projects don't work. In his research among the relatively small numbers that do, he identified a pattern for success in eight steps, shown in Figure 10.2.[7]

The inclusion of commonly accepted features of leadership, such as tenacity and vision, is no surprise, but Kotter has stressed the first step ('a sense of urgency') as being the most important to leadership of change. He cautions that, at each step, there may be pitfalls – complacency or false urgency at the

start are unproductive, a failure to build a team or an alliance
to overcome resistance to change (people tend to be very
conservative when faced with the idea of change) is another,
while organisational politics or lack of a clear vision can disrupt
a reorganisation or change project. Perhaps the most striking
aspect of this (and other change models) is its linear design.

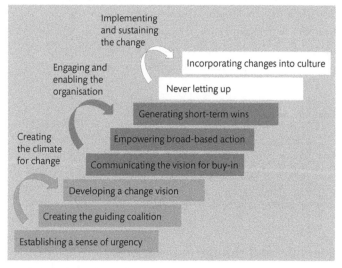

FIGURE 10.2 Kotter's eight steps of change
Source: **http://www.kotterinternational.com/our-principles/
changesteps/changesteps**, Kotter International. Reproduced with
permission.

A systems view, meanwhile, warns us to expect change to
be more fluid, turbulent and full of feedback loops (as well
as unintended consequences). Some of these aspects appear
only later, after the change agent (leader) has moved on. In
this case, putting too much store just in the persona of a
leader to deliver will result in disappointment. This brings us
back to a general theme: learning.

The organisational development (OD) movement of the last
20 years sees leadership as located throughout the system –
embedded in the 'learning organisation'. The original

influences for the term 'learning organisation' were the work of Donald Schön and Chris Argyris in the 1980s[8] and Peter Senge's influential book *The Fifth Discipline*.[9] These promoted a systems perspective but failed to challenge the non-systems dogma prevalent in all hierarchical or individualistic versions of leadership.

Good examples of challenging approaches to leadership are to be found, however, and one such is the remarkable transformation brought about on a US nuclear-powered submarine under the command of Captain David Marquet, whose crew were encouraged towards excellence rather than compliance, and away from top down leader-follower. Marquet's call to distribute empowerment and leadership by moving authority to the information, and not the other way around.

Putting it together: may the force be with you

There is a lot of overlap between leadership and management (and between leader and manager as roles), though in one respect there is a big difference. Perhaps this is the only difference that matters. Management is about trying your best to avoid nasty surprises. In all but the most trivial cases of trial and error, management does not embrace the unknown. Leadership emerges in situations where we do not know with absolute certainty what is going to happen next. And because we live in open systems, we really never know what's going to happen next.

As definition is so difficult, so perhaps we can ask instead, 'If leadership is the answer, then what was the question?' I think there are three:

1 *Who's in charge?* It flows in specific situations as agreement on from structure, hierarchy, order, or chain of command. Tasks need to be done, and we often look to a person to

exert power and organisational influence in such decision making.

2 *What could be?* It emerges from vision, connecting the dots, excitement, action (influencing through the power of ideas or thought) and passion. It can also be a call to action by circumstances.

3 *Whom shall we follow?* An acknowledgement of and connection with the deep human need to have something to believe in, and to say 'Yes, I'm in!'

Getting inside and then beyond such questions is the art. Art requires a passionate, inward commitment. Finally, be aware that success in leadership is always measured backwards and seen in hindsight – another reason to hold the concept lightly in your mind as you move forward.

QUESTIONS FOR REFLECTION

1 What is your calling? What are you passionate about? What would you do if you were free to do anything and know it would be a success?

2 What groups or communities influence you most?

Further reading

A classic text: *Good to Great* by Jim Collins (2001), Random House Business. One of the most interesting books on leadership.

Going deeper: *Leadership: Theory and Practice* (8th edition, 2018) by Peter Northouse, Sage. A very comprehensive and readable survey of the main theories of leadership.

Turn The Ship Around!: A True Story of Building Leaders by Breaking the *Rules* (2015) by David Marquet, Portfolio Penguin. An honest and rewarding account of the development of a leader-leader model on a US nuclear-powered submarine, with many great lessons for business everywhere.

The Toyota Way to Lean Leadership: Achieving and Sustaining Excellence through Leadership Development (2011) by Jeffrey Liker and Gary Convis, McGraw-Hill.

Watch this:

'Never play to the gallery' – a brief excerpt of an interview with David Bowie in which he talks about how to challenge yourself and grow: **https://youtu.be/cNbnef_eXBM**.

Notes

1 Bennis, W. and Nanus, B. (1986) *Leaders: Strategies for Taking Charge*, new edition, HarperBusiness.

2 Tzu, L. (1989) *The Complete Works of Lao Tzu*, Seven Star Communications.

3 Collins, J. (2001) *Good to Great*, Random House Business.

4 Greenleaf, R. and Spears, L. (2002) *Servant Leadership: A Journey into the Nature of Legitimate Power and Greatness*, 25th anniversary edition, Paulist Press International.

5 **Lagos, Nigeria. https://www.un.org/africarenewal/magazine/april-2019-july-2019/africa%E2%80%99s-megacities-magnet-investors. https://sites .uoit.ca/sustainabilitytoday/urban-and-energy-systems/Worlds-largest-cities/ population-projections/city-population-2050.php.**

6 Lichtenstein, B.B. and Plowman, D.A. (2009) 'The leadership of emergence: A complex systems leadership theory of emergence at successive organizational levels', *The Leadership Quarterly*, 20(4): 617–30.

7 Kotter, J. (2012) *Leading Change*, with a new preface by the author, Harvard Business Review Press.

8 Argyris, C. and Schön, D. (1995) *Organizational Learning: Theory, Method and Practice*, 2nd edition, Financial Times/Prentice Hall.

9 Senge, P. (2006) *The Fifth Discipline: The Art and Practice of the Learning Organization*, 2nd edition, Random House Business.

Entrepreneurship
Finding a gap in the market and a market in the gap

> Different parts of the world have different attitudes to failure. Arguably, it may take more courage to be an entrepreneur in Sydney, or Paris, or London, or Japan, or Singapore ... but an entrepreneur sees the world for what it could be, not what it is.[1]
>
> Guy Kawasaki

In a nutshell

New businesses that do new things don't start themselves. They begin as an idea, often in the mind of a single person, and they require time, skill, persistence and effort to get off the ground and become established. In that sense, *everyone* may be described as an entrepreneur who, whether prompted by opportunity or necessity, has ever risked something to make their business idea real. But not every small business is an entrepreneurial venture, and not every entrepreneurial venture starts life in a small company. There are some specific characteristics that describe an entrepreneurial start-up, and the entrepreneurs who make them happen.

Knowing about entrepreneurship is valuable for everyone, not just the would-be entrepreneur. The principles of entrepreneurship are good for reinvention in large, well-established companies as well and solo entrepreneurs provide the fuel for economic growth and innovation.

Entrepreneurship is too important to ignore.

In this chapter you will:

▌ examine the role played by start-ups in commerce and economic development

▌ find out what kind of person becomes an entrepreneur

▌ develop a fledgling business idea of your own

In this chapter, I encourage you to work on an entrepreneurial idea for starting something new, or doing something familiar in a new way. Put yourself in the entrepreneur's mindset as you read.

What is an entrepreneur?

An entrepreneur is a person who is motivated to find profitable ways of doing new things, or do existing things in new ways, and who turns ideas into viable businesses. Entrepreneurship is the practice of identifying such opportunities and bringing them to life, and while every new entrepreneurial venture starts small, not all small businesses are entrepreneurial. There is a difference. The entrepreneur's idea is to grow way beyond small ... and change the world (most small business owners are content not disrupting the status quo).

Anyone can be an entrepreneur, and they can be found throughout the world. In most countries, more men become entrepreneurs than women, although we must be careful how we define what an entrepreneur is. An entrepreneur is someone who has overcome resistance and many barriers to make something happen. Perhaps they did this by setting up their own organisation, perhaps within an existing one.

Studying people who choose this path gives us a little bit of theory to understand how entrepreneurship happens. One of the earliest and most influential writers on entrepreneurship was the Austrian economist *Joseph Schumpeter*. In 1934, while teaching at Harvard Business School, he published a book called *The Theory of Economic Development*, and this has been most people's starting point for talking about entrepreneurship ever since. Schumpeter saw the world as dynamic and business as cyclical; he was fascinated by the role the entrepreneur plays in many societies around the world, providing the fluidity and innovation necessary for a healthy economy. This renewing energy often comes from the bottom up, and is always disruptive of the established order.

So, to begin with, an entrepreneur is someone who:

▌ takes risks in order to create new organisations that were not there before

▌ takes a stake in the company or venture

▌ remains in a control position until the new organisation is through its initial phases and established. Being a business owner might be part of being an entrepreneur.

In many ways, entrepreneurs are setting out to answer one of the fundamental questions of leadership from the previous chapter, namely 'what could be?' Entrepreneurship means influencing and persuading others to get on board and come along for the ride.

DAY BY DAY PRACTICE

Stop for a moment and consider. Have you ever had an idea to start a new business? Spend a few minutes making some notes on what that was, in light of the things you have read in this book.

If you have never thought about this, look around you now and see if there are any gaps or opportunities for things other people might need or buy. Again, sketch some preliminary notes.

As an entrepreneur, you start out as a lone voice suggesting something new. It can be tough not just because you will be running counter to how things are now, but because you will be facing your own fear of failure and of being judged. Entrepreneurs are human. They are as emotional, thin-skinned and vulnerable to self-doubt as everyone else and fear of failure can be a real barrier. But think for a moment what this means. People are not born with fear of failure; it is a contextual and socialised concept; it is conditioned. If you live in a society that supports and values entrepreneurship, you are more likely to start a new business; failure will not stop you from having another go. If the world around commerce is punishing of failure, then few will try.

Entrepreneurs have to be careful to identify neither with success nor failure. We may all have a certain need for attention and recognition, and a wish to be in control, but it's businesses that fail or win, not the entrepreneur as a person. Were you to judge *yourself* according to whether an entrepreneurial venture is showered with plaudits and praise, or hit with criticism and condemnation, you are showing only your conditioning. Self-awareness is very important to be an entrepreneur (remember the Theranos case study? That's a great example of what happens when this is missing).

It is not a particular personality type that becomes an entrepreneur, it is acting on an idea. Of course, context can encourage people into entrepreneurship where they might otherwise have done something different, as in the following case study.

CASE STUDY

The migrant entrepreneur

In 2001, Rafael dos Santos left his native Brazil to come to the UK. With no network, almost no English, and finding his Brazilian qualifications not recognised, his twenty-first birthday was spent behind a sink washing dishes on a 12-hour trial to become a kitchen porter. 'Being a migrant is like being a child in an adult's body,' he says, 'as one is powerless to influence one's surroundings'. But a determination to succeed saw him learn the language in two years, gain friends and, in 2003, start his first business, letting flat-share rooms in London. By 2014, when he sold the company, it was employing 15 people. He then dedicated his time to help migrant entrepreneurs like himself navigate the process of start-up.

As part of his recent Executive MBA, Rafael researched the biggest barriers for start-up and growth of migrant business. They don't lack determination or acumen, he discovered, but the time it takes to settle in and build a network, the lack of funding (80 per cent of migrants fund their business with savings, friends and family borrowings or home country loans) and unfamiliarity with local business contexts all make it very hard. He found that 14 per cent of UK businesses are founded by migrants, with highest rates in the extremes of high-tech or unskilled service sectors. Perhaps because they have experienced being on the cultural and social outside, learning the business basics from scratch, migrant entrepreneurs have much to give back when they succeed. In Rafael's case, this has seen him publish his report with the Institute of Directors and set up, in 2018, an award-winning PR club called High Profile Club, which is now helping migrant entrepreneurs get featured in the media.

Success factors

An entrepreneur will appreciate the nature of risk and take what can be learnt from one venture over to the next. An entrepreneurial venture is defined as successful once it has survived its initial phase, perhaps the first two years, and the majority of new business ventures will not make it beyond this time period. A successful start-up invariably will have:

- an orientation towards and ambitions for (exponential) growth
- a willingness and perhaps a plan for an exit strategy, such as selling to or partnering with others, or new ventures launched from profits (Richard Branson's preferred model)
- the right people on the bus; the search and selection of staff who can maintain the venture's distinctive form of innovation as it grows is often crucial.

Remember, though, that none of these guarantees success because you also require favourable conditions and luck. Though they may end up giants, successful start-ups don't behave like big businesses when they begin. They require a different set of metrics to measure how they are performing and what they should do next.

Global Entrepreneurship Monitor (GEM)

Entrepreneurship will always be present when the conditions and indicators are right. One such indicator is if the rate that new businesses are coming into existence is faster than the rate they're going out of business. For example, in 2017, there were 5.7 million businesses in the UK (96 per cent of which employed fewer than 10 people). In that year, 414,000 new businesses were started – a net gain of 86,000. By contrast, in 2009, in the wake of the worldwide recession, that trend had been reversed.

The *Global Entrepreneurship Monitor* (GEM) is an annual report on the environment and climate for entrepreneurship. It was first produced by Babson College in the USA in 1998 and today it is, by far, the most influential mapping of entrepreneurship. GEM tracks trends among hundreds of thousands of solo entrepreneurs *and* employees who develop new goods and services within existing firms and in 2018 the report covered 54 countries, which account for roughly 85 per cent of global GDP. One key indicator in GEM is the percentage of adults surveyed who have started and have been running their venture for up to three and a half years, a rate known as *Total Early-Stage Entrepreneurial Activity* (TEA). The global economy is diverse, so GEM borrows three levels of economic development taken from the World Economic Forum:

▌ **Factor-driven development,** found in the least developed economies such as Vietnam and India. Here, most entrepreneurial activity is innovation in basic things like subsistence agriculture, resource extraction, public health or education. Because these are the poorest parts of the world, entrepreneurship levels are an indicator of transitions from lowest economic levels to middling ones.

▌ **Efficiency-driven development,** found wherever productivity and economic standards are already on the rise. All over the world, entrepreneurs are at work contributing to the rapid development of markets and availability of goods and services that may have been unaffordable a generation or two before. Entrepreneurs perform the vital, incremental function of getting whole systems to function more efficiently. This kind of entrepreneurship is found in South Africa, China and Mexico. In the next chapter, we will return to note the significance of this point.

▌ **Innovation-driven development** happens in mature economies, where knowledge is both source of and end-product for innovation. Entrepreneurial activity often is therefore skewed more towards the service sector and to innovation of ideas in countries such as South Korea, the United Kingdom and the USA. In these markets, innovation needs to be more disruptive before it succeeds and has an impact. As someone reading this book, the odds are that you and any business ideas you have will be at this economic level.

In all cases, access to funding, elimination of unnecessary bureaucracy and red tape, and access to appropriate exit routes will be vital. The other unifying characteristic across levels is *innovation*, so let's look at this in more detail.

Innovation

Innovation is a sub-set of creativity. It means introducing profitable products or services that other companies are not offering, and that are new to at least some customers. *Novelty*, *exclusivity* and *viability* are, therefore, pre-requisites for in-company entrepreneurial ventures or projects (perhaps making it a little bit different from R&D). Innovation is the home turf of the *intrapreneur*. Organisations that rely on innovation must give employees the same kind of freedom to work independently that the entrepreneur has, in order to come up with ideas and projects that can revitalise or diversify a business. Intrapreneurs share a lot of the same hurdles and obstacles as entrepreneurs. They, too, must communicate well and persuade others of the power (or urgency, as we'll see in Chapter 12) of their idea.

Innovation needs to be specific and classically there are five ways to frame this:

1 new goods or new services

2 new methods of making existing products or new ways of performing a service

3 finding and opening new markets

4 finding new sources of supply

5 reorganising processes or disrupting operations in such a way that it leads to measurable competitive advantage from any of the first four.

DAY BY DAY PRACTICE

1 Below are eight entrepreneurial start-ups (with country of origin). If you don't already know them, find out what sort of innovation each offered:

Uber (USA), Amazon (USA), WeWork (USA), Paytm (India), Klarna (Sweden), Deliveroo (UK), Darktrace (UK), and Ofo (China).

Do any of these tick more than one box?

2 Now revisit your business idea asked for at the start of the chapter. Can you find a home in any of the five? Is your organisation missing out on intrapreneurship?

Spotting and developing a business opportunity

Let's take a look at the business end of entrepreneurship – actions an entrepreneur takes in identifying a need or opportunity and getting a new venture off the ground. To prosper and contribute to society and make a living, entrepreneurs need to understand what in the environment is working for them and what might hold them back. Here you could use a PESTEL once more, a framework not confined just to big business strategy decisions.

The stereotype of the entrepreneur as reckless, obsessed with money and fame is almost never the case. Most are thoughtful and thorough, and diverse in character, age and background. What they have in common are two things:

1. **An ability to act quickly:** this is because they know the value of first-mover advantage but also because they've prepared.

2. **An ambition to shake things up:** entrepreneurs rarely want just to get into the game and merely grab a piece of an existing pie. Their wish is to find something with a potential that no one else has realised and make the pie bigger (or bake a new pie). They research the problem and all its existing solutions, as well as the potential from their new offering.

That wish is the easy part; then the work begins. The first step, however, is always the same – mining and then polishing a big idea. There are as many ways of coming up with a new business idea as there are people who become entrepreneurs, but three ways seem to crop up more frequently:

- **Flash of inspiration:** the bolt from the blue or spark of an idea sometimes appears, maybe with no real sense of where it came from. Inherently creative, an open mindset helps foster this.

- **Hard-working creativity:** arguably, the realm of the inventor-entrepreneur, focusing on both the art and science of being creative. The entrepreneur, not the market, is the methodical source of new ideas. With persistence and practice, this approach can pay off. Often, one idea, tested and failed, leads to another, and another, until …

▌**Opportunity from needs:** scrupulously studying a market or situational factors and mapping an unmet need, then engineering a product or service to fill it. Many entrepreneurs with industry or management experience work this way. This is, perhaps, the most relevant to *Day by Day MBA thinking* because it can draw on the knowledge and skills developed in this book. The key to finding a new business idea this way begins in educating yourself.

Opportunities are all around us if we know how to find and understand them, and this means starting with a problem. A good test for a business problem is to answer the questions below:

1 Is this a problem that really bothers people? Do people care about the issue?

2 Is this a common problem? How many people does it affect?

3 Is it feasible to do something about it?

4 Is there a solution possible that doesn't exist now?

5 Could that be turned into a business opportunity?

Do as much research as you can into the issue – its background, who it affects, who offers solutions at present and what kind of solution would shake things up.

DAY BY DAY PRACTICE

Return to the business idea you were asked to start considering at the start of the chapter. Apply some of the principles of this section to developing it and understanding what sort of entrepreneurial idea it is. Is this idea possible to start as a business on your own, or would you need partners?

Try the five questions on it. If you score 'yes' five times, then your next step could be a move into action.

Creating your business model

Now we come to that part of being an entrepreneur that most of us think of as starting a new venture. But remember, this will not be the start by any means. This section is about preparing the space for your business model while bearing in mind that your real model will be formed by the process as you go. The *Business Model Canvas* (see Figure 11.1) is a framework for strategists and entrepreneurs to do just that. It is the work of **Strategyzer.com** and is a useful tool for organising information and prioritising the types of questions, decisions and action steps that all entrepreneurs need to consider in their preparation to launch and run their new venture.

DAY BY DAY PRACTICE

Use the various elements and questions from the Business Model Canvas that follows to sketch out your idea for an entrepreneurial venture.

Key partners	Who are they? Who has a stake? What motivates them? Who creates the added value in your business? You, or your partners (e.g. suppliers)? Is the best route to market a deal or partnership with others?
Key activities	To make your value proposition real, what needs to happen?
Key resources	How protected are you (e.g. intellectual property (IP), protection via patents, first-mover advantage or branding)? Are the resources you need scarce or easy to find? At what point would this become too much for you to handle alone?
Value propositions	What need is being met (new need, or existing need in a new way)? What are customers willing to pay your offer? How will you convince them? Above all, what distinguishes you from others?

Key partners	Key activities	Value propositions	Customer relationships	Customer segments
(who you need around you to provide additional resources)	(what must be done to make all the other parts a reality)	(set out for each customer segment)	(how to get, keep and integrate customers)	(viable categories of people who might pay for your product or service)
	Key resources (what assets and financing you must have to deliver value)		Channels (how you interact with or deliver value to customers)	
Cost structure (an idea of what costs you generate in delivering value)			Revenue streams (pricing and descriptions of mechanisms that generate cash flow)	

FIGURE 11.1 Business Model Canvas

Customer segments	Who is your customer? Who else is in this market? Who else could enter easily?
Customer relations	What kind of relationship are you and they looking for? What would stand in the way of them leaving you?
Channels	How are you going to reach your customer(s)?
Cost structure	How expensive are your costs of sales? What is your margin? How will these change as you scale up? Can you 'bootstrap' (cover all your own start-up costs) or do you need to seek financing?
Revenue streams	Transactional and one-off, or recurring and repeat business? When will you receive payment? One of the most commons reason start-ups fail is that they run out of cash, so can you remain solvent with expected cash flows?

The Business Model Canvas offers these in no particular order, although you will probably start with 'Value proposition' and 'Customer segments' before considering other elements. Don't expect the perfect formula, or even perfect answers to any of these questions because successful entrepreneurs don't all follow the same path or prioritise the same things. For the intrapreneur, an adapted version may also be a useful exercise. Resources available *within* an organisation may be huge, yet new ideas can be killed off by internal resistance or politics.

Lean start-up

The *lean start-up* embraces the imperfect and pared down business model and is an approach usually associated with Eric Ries, a US entrepreneur and author. Lean start-ups are favoured by young entrepreneurs in innovation-driven economies where information technology or software products dominate. They follow an iterative, trial and error path where the business plan is a constantly evolving, living document rather than a blue-print. Doing it this way really helps control costs and minimise the risks of long lead-times to market launch in fast-moving industries. In fact, lean start-ups aim openly to release what Ries calls a *minimum viable product* quickly by involving key early customers during the planning process. Your business model *is* learning from this (expecting failure and set-back) and, if necessary, *pivoting* (changing course) in a way that keeps your original purpose. This business model is, therefore, the *result* of the start-up, not its cause. Done well, the new organisation remains ready to move, change or adapt very quickly as it grows because with all this proto-typing you are not cemented to a heavy foundation. Versions of the Business Model Canvas have been adapted to the lean start-up and reflect the focus on iterations of testing and customer feedback. Some criticism has been made of the method because of its readiness to cut resources to control costs, and clearly not every type of new idea can afford to produce repeated prototypes if the customer expects a polished product. In any case, lean start-ups still require the right ecosystem to flourish, so we are not dealing with a magic formula that will work in every context.

Social entrepreneurship

Social entrepreneurship is a category of business that returns us to an enduring theme of this book, namely that there is a link between individual health and well-being and that of the group or community, and that of the environment (see the next chapter for more on this). Social entrepreneurship is a rapidly growing form of new venture, with most such activity happening in the USA, Australia, Western Europe (roughly 11 per cent in each case), and in sub-Saharan Africa (9 per cent). Economic policy is one way of encouraging economic goals with more than just profit in mind and, according to GEM, about one-third of all entrepreneurial ventures in the world rely on government funding.

In contexts where the economic base level is low, all entrepreneurship is, to some extent, social entrepreneurship because it has the effect of improving the life conditions of the whole community. Roughly equal numbers of social entrepreneurs are men and women, which is not the case with commercial entrepreneurship. They're generally younger, too.

QUESTIONS FOR REFLECTION

1 What's the most entrepreneurial thing you've done in your career? How did it go? Why?

2 As a manager or leader, generally, when you ask people at work questions, is it because you want them to understand you, or because you want to understand them? Be honest.

Further reading

A classic text: *The Entrepreneur: Classic Texts by Joseph A. Schumpeter* (2011), by Thorbjorn Knudsen, Markus Becker and Richard Swedberg, Stanford Business Books. Collected works from Schumpeter's career.

Going deeper: *Entrepreneurship* (2015, 5th edition) by Bruce Barringer and Duane Ireland, global edition, Pearson. A comprehensive and mainstream overview that can act as a handy reference to dip into.

Global Entrepreneurship Monitor (GEM) offers archived, in-depth reports and resources to help you understand the context and macro trends in entrepreneurship: **www.gemconsortium.org**.

Watch these:	Watch Amazon founder Jeff Bezos talk about the many things that Amazon does, and how their guiding principles of customer obsession, willingness to invent, experiment and fail in the right way, and 'long-term thinking': **https://www.youtube.com/watch?v=KPbKeNghRYE**.
	Made for general entertainment, *Dragons' Den* does deliver an education on occasion, too. The clip of how Scottish tech start-up **Beezer.com** secured Peter Jones as their investor illustrates the principles and spirit of this chapter very well: **https://www.insider.co.uk/news/dragons-den-beezer-peter-jones-13164460**.

Note

1 Guy Kawasaki quoted from 2015 article on **Mashable.com**: https://mashable
.com/2015/05/05/guy-kawasaki-apple-watch/#xhwVNRBynaqj.

Sustainability
Glass half full or glass half empty?

I always make the business case for sustainability. It's so compelling. Our costs are down, not up. Our products are the best they have ever been. Our people are motivated by a shared higher purpose – esprit de corps to die for. And the goodwill in the marketplace – it's just been astonishing.

Ray C. Anderson, founder of Interface Inc.

In a nutshell

Business has many challenges, but arguably none is more important than the pressing social and environmental questions facing us today. This chapter offers an overview of some topics that are now finding their way on to MBA curricula, and that are all intrinsically visionary in their nature. For organisations to endure over time, they must achieve two things. First, they need stability and, second, they need change (you cannot have one without the other). So far, this is nothing new, and there is much in all the strategic thinking explored in Part 3 that deals with this. The difference now is that the context of stability and change is not confined only to the organisation's internal and external environment, but to the context of the environment itself. Many businesses have been aware of this for some time, and some have pioneered a more radical business model, but most have restricted active change to support for social issues and development of more conscientious policies that mitigate the impact of commercial activity on the planet.

Managers used to be taught in Business Schools that *sustainability* meant guaranteeing growth. Nowadays, flowing from responsibility and ethical leadership, sustainability deals with perpetuity, or long-term survival in terms of the relationship every business has with its immediate environment. Beginning in *corporate social responsibility*, many organisations now align their beliefs, if not their missions, to a contribution to social progress and limiting the damage they do to the environment. What is new and urgent is how this is not enough. We risk ending with the relationship we all have as a species with the biosphere as a whole, permanently.

Changing to a sustainable business model needs foresight, courage and the ethical compass of wisdom. It needs leadership in order to make sure that there is a legacy for the following generations to enjoy.

In this chapter you will:

▌ define corporate social responsibility in management

▌ define sustainability

▌ ask how organisations should act to manage the issues faced

Why you should take this seriously

There is mounting evidence that human activity is directly influencing climate and biosphere. It is not going unnoticed. One indication of this can be found in the annual Global Risks Report published by the World Economic Forum (WEF). Policy makers and business practitioners are surveyed and risks aggregated in two separate rankings, one for likelihood and the other for impact.[1] For 2008, the year of the economic crash that ushered in global recession, and then for 2018, the top five looked like this:

Top 5 global risks in terms of likelihood		Top 5 global risks in terms of impact	
2008	2018	2008	2018
Asset price collapse (Economic)	Extreme weather events (Environmental)	Asset price collapse (Economic)	Weapons of mass destruction (Geopolitical)
Middle East uncertainty (Geopolitical)	Natural disasters (Environmental)	Retrenchment from globalisation (in developed economies) (Geopolitics)	Extreme weather events (Environmental)
Failed and falling states (Geopolitical)	Cyberattacks (Technological)	Slowing Chinese economy (Economic)	Natural disasters (Environmental)
Oil and gas price spike (Economic)	Data fraud or theft (Technological)	Oil and gas price spike (Economic)	Oil and gas price spike (Environmental)
Chronic disease (in developed economies) (Societal)	Failure of climate change and mitigation (Environmental)	Pandemics (Societal)	Water crises (Societal)

In 2008, you can see how dominant were economics and geopolitics, the familiar ground of strategic thinking (and theories). The situation has been shifting and by 2018 the survey reveals a different picture. Risks around a reliance on advanced computing technology isn't a surprise, but the list is dominated by outcomes that are not under our direct control. Threats are no longer about relative competitive advantage; they are existential. Doing more of the same is not an option.

DAY BY DAY PRACTICE

If you have been following the practice activities in this book, you may know a lot more about the history and set up of your organisation, how it measures value, what its culture is like and, perhaps, what its strategy is for the next business cycle. It's probable that your company has a statement on its relationship with the environment. It's much less likely that it has changed its business model.

Where does your organisation stand on:

1 social justice?

2 impact on the environment?

3 sustainable development goals?

Can you think of any companies that you would describe as 'green'? How do they differ from yours?

Before we look at sustainability as a topic for future generations, let's look at how far management thinking has developed to date.

Corporate social responsibility (CSR)

Concern for how companies do business are not new and often are represented by a concept known as corporate social responsibility, or CSR. Definitions vary but generally it is agreed that CSR:

▌ is voluntary but goes above and beyond the legal minimum

▌ takes into account multiple and wide-ranging stakeholders, not just shareholders and customers

▌ internalises external impacts; CSR brings in-house the
  effects and costs of corporate activity that might otherwise
  be met by the community (e.g. the results of waste products
  on the environment) but doesn't necessarily eliminate the
  impact itself

▌ is about more than corporate philanthropy; the
  conventional image for CSR (see Carroll's pyramid in
  Figure 12.1) has been one of organisations donating funds
  to or promoting charitable projects, not making social
  progress a part of every internal business function.

FIGURE 12.1 Carroll's hierarchy of CSR aims
Source: Adapted from Carroll, A.B. (1991) 'The pyramid of corporate social
responsibility: Toward the moral management of organizational stakeholders',
Business Horizons, 34(4): 39–48. Reproduced with permission of Elsevier.

Most for-profit organisations would go along with these
points. Where it becomes contentious is in the next point,
namely that CSR:

▌ does not put social responsibilities above economic ones.
  This economic principle underpins the others.

It may also, of course, undermine them. Companies often
need to make a business case for CSR. What is the business

case for CSR? Let's start with an influential economist and see what Milton Friedman had to say on this subject:

> There is one and only one social responsibility of business – to use its resources and engage in activities designed to increase its profits so long as it stays within the rules of the game, which is to say, engages in open and free competition without deception or fraud.[2]

Friedman rejects the idea that an organisation has a moral purpose beyond the interests of the individuals who own it. A manager's only duty, he seems to say, is to pursue profit, presumably in the belief that they can then use their wealth to better society generally. Whoever wants to put a case for CSR must, therefore, have an answer to Friedman's bold statement. Where Friedman saw no justification for anything beyond the healthy creation of profit, others have concluded that a definition of CSR cannot be restricted to profit maximisation. There are two reasons why CSR could be a requirement:

1. If every person has a moral duty to act in an ethical way, then so does every organisation (because an organisation is an individual in the eyes of the law). The problem with this is that managers are supposed to represent shareholder interests, so when does corporate responsibility override fiduciary duty? Do managers have the authority to think or act on wider social problems without knowing whether this is what the shareholders would do?

2. Alternatively, if an organisation exists only because it is part of a bigger, wider system that creates a social imperative to act in an ethical manner, then managers have a moral duty to put this interest first.

The problem, according to Henry Mintzberg, is that managers are not equipped to act with CSR principles in mind.[3] Managers are promoted to senior positions on the basis of their proven ability as experts in creating value, not on their understanding of wider social issues. The fear is that, if corporations are driven to seek only competitive advantage, they are more likely in their actions to create social problems than solve them.

How far does this change the general direction beyond the boundary of the organisation? Is this changing? As a manager, CSR brings you into contact once more with values and beliefs, which we met in a personal context in Chapter 2. One problem for CSR being more than window-dressing is the difference between what people at the top say they believe and what they actually require the people in the middle to do. If these are not the same, and especially if middle management performance is tied to short-term financial goals, then any statement of CSR can look to the outside world like 'greenwash'. Often it can take real courage and vision in a senior manager to intervene in the 'business-as-usual' mentality strongly enough to apply principles that, at first, don't appear to contribute to the traditional bottom line.

DAY BY DAY PRACTICE

Does your organisation have a statement or a position on CSR? If so, have you looked at it? Try to identify the assumptions used in its construction. If not, would this be a good exercise for your organisation?

Triple bottom line

Strategic decisions have social as well as economic consequences and many companies have in the last 10 years begun to devote much more time and energy to CSR. Measuring this, though, has never been easy. In 1994, John Elkington published a landmark book, *Cannibals with Forks*, kicking off a worldwide movement to quantify the aims of the United Nations in promoting sustainable development.[4]

Elkington introduced the term *triple bottom line* (3BL)
to illustrate his point. The bottom line has long been a
euphemism for the financial performance of an organisation
and a metaphor for the success or not of a business. That
financial aspect is covered in Elkington's model by 'profits', to
which 'people' and 'planet' are new additions (see Figure 12.2).

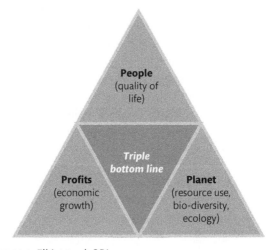

FIGURE 12.2 Elkington's 3BL

The relationship between people and profits needs to be
equitable, while between people and planet it needs to
be bearable, and between profits and planet it must be
viable. Where these three meet, says the theory, is called
'sustainable', a theme explored more in a moment.

The Base of the Pyramid

The Base of the Pyramid refers to the approximately 3–4
billion people in the world who live at an economic level
significantly lower than the 1 billion people who live in
the 'mature' countries, where needs and wants are largely
met. It was first put forward by two economic strategists,
C.K. Prahalad and Stuart Hart.[5] The base is the 'survival

economy' – where meeting daily needs is a struggle and where billions of people live on just a few dollars a day. Yet the Base is also a massive business opportunity, full of local vigour, innovation and entrepreneurial promise. There is potential, too, for an entirely new economic model based on alternatives or variants of capitalism. Sitting between the Base and the peak is an aspiring middle class of at least 2 billion people whose needs are now being met, but whose wants will, inevitably, put further pressure on a delicate ecosystem. The middle of the pyramid attracts the majority of the Foreign Direct Investment (FDI) and other investment by MNEs and is likely to continue to be an extension of existing technology.

DAY BY DAY PRACTICE

Visit **TED.com** and watch the Hans Rosling talk entitled 'The magic washing machine': **https://www.ted.com/talks/ hans_rosling_and_the_magic_washing_machine**.[6] This is one of several engaging TED talks Rosling gave. How would you describe his worldview? How does it compare with yours?

The Base has been ignored largely by MNEs except in philanthropic gestures. Any organisation with a business model addressing this segment is synonymous with the pyramid Base itself. 'Mature world' business models will not work at the Base, so the poor are not just another source of consumer demand to meet in the same way that we have described in earlier chapters. The market is for goods or services that are sustainable at that level. Without question, the keys to economic emancipation at the Base include elements such as education and control of the reproductive process by women, as these are the only proven routes for a population out of poverty. Economic activity that promotes sustainable livelihoods is a long-term, holistic and socially responsible investment, and needs to work respectfully with the vitality and innovation often driving the desire for a better life.

CSR and its offshoots are developed market phenomena and are handy templates for aligning an organisation's efforts, but it is now clear that these expressions of concern for the environment are being superseded by growing calls for an entirely new and radically different business model. Around the world, there have been a growing number of examples of people and organisations working to a business agenda subtly different from the established shareholder value model. These include social partnerships that enable NGOs, not-for-profits and businesses to work together on societal or environmental collaboration with for-profits, cooperatives and Fairtrade Foundation initiatives (in 2017, sales of Fairtrade products in the UK were £1.64 billion). This brings us to an idea that is now emerging as a serious attempt to look at the ecological, sociological and economic challenges facing us.

Sustainability

Sustainability is one of the hot topics in business. The globalised business model we know in the developed and developing world has been built on a presupposition of growth and unrestrained access to natural resources, which our technology is designed to continue to find new ways to exploit. This is a deep-rooted cultural attitude, informed by scientific methods and political ideals that have incrementally provided wealth creation and social change for 200 years. But it wasn't until 1987 that the UN World Commission on Environment and Development (the Brundtland Commission) called for all of us to make development sustainable:

> to ensure that it meets the needs of the present generation without compromising the ability of future generations to meet their own needs.[7]

There are three sorts of inter-linked change, driving an interest in sustainability at the macroeconomic level:

▌ **Demographic:** changes in size and form of the world's population, including divisions based on relative levels of equality and poverty (1.2 billion people live in extreme poverty). These changes include an ageing population, falling rates of child mortality, falling birth rate and a peak in world population of about 9.8 billion by 2050 and 11 billion by 2100.[8] Future world population growth is going to be dominated by nine countries. Globally, birth rates will always fall as economies lift themselves out of poverty, and both education and business acumen will play a huge role in this. In many developed economies, the issue is one of ageing populations. Younger people (human capital) are needed to work and fund the costs of paying pensions, and improvements in diet and health care mean that people are living much longer than their forebears. All the market and business mechanics that *MBA Day by Day* covers will need to change to adjust to these facts. For everyone in the world to achieve a North American economic profile would be well beyond the capacity of our resources in the way we currently consume or value them.

▌ **Ecosystems:** an ecosystem is defined by the OECD as 'a system in which the interaction between different organisms and their environment generates a cyclic interchange of materials and energy'.[9] I think this is a bit dry, and not the full story. When you think about it, the organisation you work for has its own micro-ecosystem with materials and energy, but these don't define it. Ecosystems are really about patterns of relationship. The cyclic interchange is actually one of information, and it's those complex sets of relationships that you manage. Our major ecosystems are dynamic and, over time, naturally exhibit variations in biodiversity and resource availability. In all the three types, (terrestrial, aquatic and atmospheric) they are coming under extreme and rapid pressure.

Ecosystems are affected by how we use and preserve land and natural habitats, how we govern and control access to fresh water (less than 1 per cent of the water on the planet is fresh water that is accessible to us, and nearly all human economic activity requires it), how we treat the oceans and how we understand biodiversity.

▌ **Climate:** again, although our planet has seen patterns and cycles of change before, evidence of positive feedback loops contributing to global warming are overwhelming and alarming. There is consensus that this is being accelerated by the presence of greenhouse gases and other accelerants and that human activity is at least a contributory factor. To quantify the size of our carbon economy, take a look at a website called **trillionthtonne.org**, which has a running total of the estimated cumulative emissions from fossil fuel use from the beginning of the industrial era. Currently, the site predicts us reaching the one trillion tonnes mark in 2035 at the latest.

DAY BY DAY PRACTICE

Climate crisis is a business issue.

Do you agree?

Can it be tackled in a way that preserves economic growth? Examine how this question is being discussed in your organisation. If it's not, then do you think that will change?

Sustainable development is political, economic and social. It encompasses resource planning and strategy just as much as values, mission and vision statements. In the same vein, because of the suggestion that current business practices may be contributing directly to the three types of crises above, a new type of leadership or management thinking – perhaps a whole new way of understanding business – may be required. Here are three of these challenges:

▌ **Sustainable consumption:** managing supply and demand to ensure basic needs are met and quality of life maintained while minimising the use of natural, non-renewable resources and controlling emissions of waste and pollutants.

▌ **Sustainable production:** management of the supply chain within ecological limits to maintain biodiversity and regeneration and – ethically – avoid the exploitation of populations or people.

▌ **Sustainable development:** in systems thinking, no system can be understood except in terms of the larger system of which it is a part. Sustainable development has proven difficult to define because our ability accurately to predict the future has been so poor.

Interface Inc.

By the mid-1990s, US carpet tile manufacturer Interface, established in 1973 by Ray Anderson, had grown into a profitable, billion-dollar business and market leader. Around the time corporate social responsibility was becoming a buzzword for its customers, Interface sales managers convened to discuss how to respond. They asked Anderson to kick things off with his environmental vision. Interface was a classic, linear 'take-make-waste' manufacturer, and he realised he did not have one.

Anderson chanced upon Paul Hawken's book *The Ecology of Commerce*, which proposed that the success of our industrial economic model was also leading to destruction of the environment needed to sustain it. One quote in particular struck home ('like a spear in the chest'), namely 'the death of birth' as the irreversible loss of habitat and   ▶

species threatened ecological extinction. He realised that Interface was fundamentally part of the problem, not the solution. This epiphany led him, at 60, to set his company and its employees an audacious and radical challenge to own up to having got it wrong, and then lead by example away from petroleum products; no small matter for a product manufactured from synthetic materials. It also had to be done in a way that kept the business profitable. 'Mission Zero' was the goal by 2020, the goal of no negative impact on the environment through the development of a completely sustainable, closed-loop business model.

Nothing is wasted in natural ecosystems, so Interface asked itself what a carpet tile company would look like if it were designed by nature. In 1995, it started a scheme called QUEST, which gets staff to eliminate waste, including in its administration, and adopted what it calls Eco-metrics to measure progress and innovation along the way. The vision was big, but the method was measured and meticulous, always with the bottom line in view. Costs dropped and profits increased and, while some initiatives worked beyond expectation, others failed completely. Yet the core idea of moving away from extractive, *take-make-waste* to being restorative remained. By 2017, the company could say that since 1996 its carbon footprint had dropped 66 per cent, GHG emissions had fallen 96 per cent, raw materials for products had gone from 1 per cent to 56 per cent from recycled or sustainable sources, 88 per cent of its energy is bought from renewable suppliers, and a 91 per cent reduction of waste going to landfill.

Interface has had three CEOs. Ray Anderson, who died in 2011 (1973–2001), Daniel Hendrix (2001–2017) and Jay Gould (from 2017). Gould announced in November 2018 that Interface was now carbon neutral. So, what next? On track for Mission Zero, Interface has launched a new target called 'Climate Take Back', which aims to make it carbon negative, with a positive effect on the environment of its business through a new philosophy of waste-make-retake.

How do you reorganise and transform as radically without destroying the thing your shareholders want to preserve? This is a real problem faced by everyone who finds themselves drawn to a position of change leadership. Ray Anderson's discovery was that opposition to change, whether an employee, customer or shareholder, must be met 'one mind at a time', in order to establish trust.

Trust

Trust is an interesting aspect of sustainability and change. We all know what trust is – until, that is, we are asked to define it. As an idea, trust is found in every human culture. It may be identified in different ways in different places, and prized in some business models while not prized in others, but when an organisation doesn't meet the expectations of one of its key stakeholder groups, this qualifies as a risk to reputation. Trust and risk are closely related concepts. Both speculate into the future from the present, both are influenced by perceptions of the past and both involve the management of expectations.

Trust is your willingness to accept the risk that whatever you propose or are involved in could go wrong. When a manager assesses this, they should do so in terms of a stakeholder's perception of the person or organisation. The questions to ask are:

▌ **Ability:** can they?

▌ **Intention:** do they want to?

▌ **Integrity:** do they hold similar values to give us a platform for resolving any disputes?

Trust is the lubricant for cooperation and economic progress.

QUESTIONS FOR REFLECTION

1 Has your definition of what a customer is for your organisation's activity changed?

2 Should company leaders be accountable for any unintended consequences of what their organisations achieve?

3 What, in your opinion, is the over-arching purpose of business?

Putting it together: the circular economy

'Sustainable' used to mean working out how an organisation or industry could continue to grow at an acceptable rate (with an acceptable rate of return) reaching out into the future. Seventy years of management effort has gone into promoting and protecting the rights of individuals, firms and whole economies to do what was necessary to take larger slices of the pie. As long as the pie could grow, this approach worked but now we must adapt. Sustainability pulls the future, and our responsibility to take action, into the here and now. You are either managing with a sustainable business model, now or you are not.

As mature economies continue to consume unsustainable levels of resources, and as growing ones demand the right to lift people out of poverty, our current model will bring serious unintended consequences. Managing this switch to a restorative way of doing business demands visionary leadership. Perhaps an alternative form of governance in the future will be called stewardship rather than leadership. Perhaps it sees a commitment to the concept of the circular economy, which is the removal by design of the waste in a process or system. The goal is to regenerate the natural systems we rely on for life, without rejecting the idea of wealth creation or technological progress. It does, though, change the parameters of how value is created.

QUESTIONS FOR REFLECTION

1 Construct a stakeholder map of your career position. Who has an interest in or an expectation of you? Where should you put your time and energy?

2 Revisit the management roles discussed in Chapter 1. Do you see any to which you need to pay special attention in the future?

Further reading

A classic text:
The Ecology of Commerce: A declaration of sustainability by Paul Hawken (2010), Harper Paperbacks. One of the more influential books to have emerged from the sustainability movement.

Going deeper:
Factfulness: Ten Reasons We're Wrong About the World – and Why Things Are Better than You Think, by Hans Rosling, Ola Rosling and Anna Rosling Ronnlund (2018), Sceptre. A superb and uplifting account of how and why we have a distorted view of the facts.

The United Nations Sustainable Development Goals, an ambitious and wide-ranging set of targets for 2030: **https://www .un.org/sustainabledevelopment/ sustainable-development-goals/**.

Watch this:
'Let's go all-in on sustainability', a 2013 TED talk in which IKEA sustainability expert Steve Howard reports on why and how his company is responding to the challenge: **https://www.ted.com/ talks/steve_howard_let_s_go_all_in_on_ selling_sustainability?language=en**.

Notes

1 https://www.weforum.org/reports/the-global-risks-report-2018.

2 Milton Friedman, 'The social responsibility of business is to increase its profits', *The New York Times Magazine*, 13 September 1970, © The New York Times Company.

3 Mintzberg, H. (1983) 'The case for corporate social responsibility', *Journal of Business Strategy*, 4(2): 3–15.

4 Elkington, J. (1999) *Cannibals with Forks: Triple Bottom Line of 21st Century Business*, Capstone.

5 Prahalad, C.K. (2007) *The Fortune at the Bottom of the Pyramid: Eradicating Poverty Through Profits*, Wharton School Publishing.

6 Rosling was a Swedish statistician and population expert with a very engaging presentation style.

7 World Commission on Environment and Development (1987) *Our Common Future*, Oxford University Press.

8 https://www.un.org/development/desa/publications/world-population-prospects-the-2017-revision.html.

9 Glossary of Environment Statistics, Studies in Methods, Series F, No. 67, United Nations, New York, 1997.

13

'Just start walking'
A blueprint for lifelong learning

The most sublime act is to set another before you. If the fool would persist in his folly he would become wise. Folly is the cloke of knavery.

William Blake (from 'The Marriage
of Heaven or Hell')

In a nutshell

Business consultants sometimes think management academics overcomplicate the world. Academics think consultants oversimplify it. This leaves you, the practitioner, in the middle, needing to get on with your job but also aware that there are limits to your abilities and knowledge. How do you make sense of it all? In *MBA Day by Day* my aim has been to present an informed and selective overview of the content and thinking you would find at a business school and to suggest that applying those concepts also involves an evolution in your own thinking. You have been given practical prompts to apply ideas in your management practice along the way. A lot of these have suggested you talk to and share with others, and this is very important because the dialogue is part of the learning. You've also been challenged to think about your work in a more reflective way and I hope you have attempted to apply this curiosity to your daily job. As you grow your career, an enquiring mind could be the most important asset you possess.

The title of this chapter comes from a personal insight I had while in Tokyo writing this edition of the book. Japan is an advanced economy with a lifestyle and language drawing on cultural traditions very different from my own. There were two ways to learn. First I could follow a guidebook and solicit information from people who had been here before me. Although this gives plenty of shortcuts, I would be starting with other people's maps. Or, I could be an explorer and construct my own map. I chose the second. I resolved, as much as possible, not to have a precise destination and just start walking. A city and its people revealed themselves as I went, but really I ended up mapping myself. This is a good metaphor for MBA thinking and your personal development. You get to see how many assumptions and prejudices you carry around with you. An open mind also needs to be a mind empty of certainty (sometimes, this is called the beginner's mind). In my case, it led to further questions about my work as a teacher and facilitator.

In this final chapter you will:

▌ reconnect with the essential elements of business

▌ boost your management thinking for the future

▌ try a sequence of personal change activities

▌ ponder some ideas for becoming a (more) reflective and integrated leader

Career opportunities

From the outside, your career can resemble a smooth and graceful swan on a river. Under the surface, however, it can be a different story. Stress, burn-out, self-doubt and fear of failure can mean that the cost, in terms of health and well-being is high. Mid-career managers and leaders often face limits to their career progression. Some of these are easy to identify. For example:

▌ Success at one level brings promotion to another, with more responsibility, but you find your success goalposts shifted to meet everyone's expectations of commitment and achievement.

▌ Success at one level brings no promotion at all. Others may be judgemental and discriminatory, and businesses are often short-sighted.

▌ Success is suddenly redefined around you. The business environment is constantly and rapidly changing, and it is necessary to keep refreshing knowledge and skills just to keep up, but no one knows for sure what's coming along next.

Notice anything that these have in common? None of them is under your control. Pinning your self-worth to these outcomes is bound to end in failure. Then there are limits which, because they are to do with how to choose to be in the world, are very much under your control. Here are some:

▌ Your feelings of doubt or inadequacy about your current position.

▌ Your struggle to reconcile endless dilemmas about how you balance work, home, health and well-being.

▌ Your personal expectations as to what levels of commitment and achievement are good enough.

▌ Self-limiting beliefs that you may no longer even realise you carry around with you.

Fulfilling potential, gaining joy from a passion or finding purpose while maintaining balance and well-being should be your aim. And yet a lot of managers are not fulfilled. Management education (going back to school) can provide a boost to a manager's professional identity and ability as a leader because it activates personal development. Of course, as I've mentioned, the majority of working managers don't get that chance.

What can be done?

Well, quite a lot, but there are two aspects to consider. The first is your relationship to the job of management and business, and the second is your relationship to learning and change. Let's look at both, starting with management.

Management: the empty space

To get at the question of what restrains you at work, strip away everything you possibly can to reveal the essentials. In 1968, British theatre director Peter Brook wrote a short book about acting, called *The Empty Space.* Here is an extract:

> I can take any empty space and call it a bare stage. A man walks across this empty space whilst someone is watching him, and this is all that is needed for an act of theatre to be engaged. Yet when we talk about theatre this is not quite what we mean. Red curtains, spotlights, blank verse, laughter, darkness, these are all confusedly superimposed in a messy image covered by one all-purpose word.[1]

Brook's intention was to strip away all the thinking about our concept 'theatre' in order to find its essential, minimum components – an empty space, an actor and an audience. That's it. According to Brook, nothing should be added unless it adds to the situation. Be wary, he says, of the temptation to add ornament without getting the basics right.

Is thinking this way useful to your management practice? Yes, it's vital. Management is a noisy topic and if you want to understand it, you need to strip it of its ornaments and pretensions. When you get down to those basics, I think you'll find three things:

1 **A need:** the 'empty space' of business. The unmet need is a positive space, full of potential, but it must be (i)

conceivable (it can be met and without losing money) and (ii) morally acceptable (in that society).

2 **A consumer:** a consumer is implied by the need.

3 **A provider:** a provider is implied by the consumer.

Over time, we have added much decoration to these basics (the MBA is guilty of ornament, too) but at its heart management is the deliberate and purposeful orchestration of these foundational and unchanging inter-relationships. There are many skills you will develop in your career and in the jobs you hold choosing among conflicting options for ideas, resources and actions takes knowledge and experience. You'll need honesty, a strong work ethic, flexibility and mental agility and a lot of other things, that's true, but remember the fundamental nature of what business is, what an organisation is, and what role work is playing in your life. You have a relationship with your job that probably extends beyond the paper contract. Everyone who works has a relationship with their work. We often ignore this, and rarely enquire into the social web that many of us rely on for our self-esteem.

Learning to change your mind

Without doubt, what will bring you most mastery in your career is self-awareness. Self-awareness is what you reach when you truly understand your relationship with learning and change. When managers devote time to reflection and personal development and embrace change in themselves, they often begin to see change happening naturally in other people around them. Only two things in your life are completely within your control:

1 what you think and feel

2 the actions you take as a result.

Everything else, including other people's opinions of you, is *not*. Trying to change this reality is foolish.

There are three things that self-awareness, learning and change have in common. First, *awareness*. You cannot deal with or change what you have not noticed, and we rarely understand the assumptions behind our thoughts and feelings. Feel negative, or like an imposter, that everyone is judging you and seeing everything you do?[2] These feelings are in *you*, not in other people or events. We just don't see it (often we don't want to). Second, *acknowledgment*. The starting point for change is not that you agree *with* everything, but that you agree *to* it, just as it is right now. Accept that reality is just as it is. Third, *reframing*. As Shakespeare has Hamlet saying, 'There is nothing either good or bad but thinking makes it so'. Standing back from the feeling in order to observe it allows it to pass of its own accord, as thoughts do. When your attachment to acceptance or rejection and your need to be desired is relinquished, in terms of evaluating your happiness, you are free. At this point, you may just find when you give up trying to fix everything, things start to fix themselves.

As you read the next section, practise the art of identifying your thoughts and emotions, without judging them, simply seeing them as they are.

TASK FOR CHANGE (1 OF 4)

For each of the four change tasks in this chapter, note down the following:

1 How you feel beforehand.

2 How you feel during.

3 What (if any) is the reaction of those around you.

4 How you feel after.

Task 1

In the next three or four days, eat one new food and drink one new drink.

Try to make these foodstuffs you would *never* normally eat or drink. Even better, get a friend to choose a new food or drink for you to try.

Four key lessons for your management future

MBA Day by Day is a start. If you have read this book in anticipation of future study, or a move further into management, then notice which chapters or ideas most caught your attention – and dig deeper yourself. If you have read this to refresh your thinking after graduating with your own MBA, then hook back into the excitement of your course – and continue your journey.

I offer the ideas to support your further development. Each statement below is also an activity for reflective practice.

1 You won't learn how to manage an organisation in a classroom

In management, the right way to grow is by applying practice to theory. But first you need the practice. There is no substitute for being in the workplace if you want to learn the ropes in management. There are many managers who have done an MBA in their mid to late 20s who suspect that, if they had waited another 5 or 10 years, they would have got a lot more out of it. Organisations are the collective efforts of human beings – a frustrating, complicated, complex and wonderful resource – and learning how to manage them is a contact sport. Master the basics, get the experience and earn your stripes first.

The classroom can, however, be a great place to learn something about yourself. If you can combine the self-reflection of learning with others to the application of method and theory to your management experience (especially your management mistakes), you may see some dramatic results in your career. Of course, even without access to the business school classroom, you can still find many ways to learn (see the final section in this chapter for an example of a method for this).

2 There is no limit to learning

You can never be 'full' of knowledge and it is impossible to run out of things to learn. This is because the nature of knowledge is not cumulative, it is relational. For many, the truth of 'the more I know, the more there is to know' first comes as a bit of a shock, but it is then quite liberating. Think about what this means to you in your management practice and career and then consider that the biggest opportunity for personal development is open to you as you get older and more experienced. All you need is to be curious, awake and rigorous in your thinking. This may require a real change in you. If you want to do an MBA, spend time researching the school and speak to its students and alumni. Every school is different, so it's about finding the right course for you. If you have the workplace as your classroom, speak to and learn from the experience of everyone around you, regardless of rank, role or reputation.

3 Your future career is not written in your past (or your future)

I think this is huge. Most of us don't realise it, though. We like to hold on to a sense of where we have come from – it's an important part of maintaining an identity – but a lot of us sleepwalk our way through life never realising that we only actually live it in the present.

Carl Jung said that the purpose of the second half of our lives is to understand the first. I don't start the MBA Personal Development module at Henley with career goals. Rather, we begin with a guided exploration of students' life stories. This is not because they should use the past to determine the future. Quite the contrary – I do it so that they can, eventually, be free from the degree of control that they let their past have over them. From here, we can really start to explore liberating goals.

4 In the end, what matters is working things out for yourself

My fourth lesson is a hope that you will come to see for yourself things as they actually are. If you want total freedom to act, this will come only from within you, not from a doctrine. When you start work, the structure and purpose of business and management are given to you. Expertise in management comes from validation of practice. Freedom in management comes when you no longer use or need validation. When you accept, without question, the tools, methods and even theories of others in your work, you are taking for granted whatever they took for granted.

TASK FOR CHANGE (2 OF 4)

Remembering to make notes as in the first, here is the next one ...

Task 2

In the next three or four days, make a noticeable change in the layout of your surroundings.

This could be a physical movement of furniture or space around home or in the office.

Learning about yourself is different from all the other types of learning you may encounter, either at work or on an MBA. Knowledge of the self is always what's available in the present moment, while knowledge of theories, concepts, habits, and ways and means to achieve ends is always built from the past, accumulated. There is no acquisition when it comes to self-knowledge and awareness because it is an open process, constantly alert and sensitive to the world you are in.

You are unlikely to find this out during an MBA, or just from reading a book. The final part of an MBA usually includes a piece of management research or a larger strategy project. It is often where a few things fall into place, including a much stronger sense of self-confidence and critical thinking skills. Even without that, if you can find more flow and happiness at work, if you can build resilience and develop a passion for what you do, and if you can understand something of the wider social context of being a manager, then you will have succeeded in starting a very worthwhile journey.

TASK FOR CHANGE (3 OF 4)

Remembering to make notes as in the first and second, here is the next one ...

Task 3

In the next three or four days, change something about your image or social identity.

Make it something that is new for *you*, and the only rule is that it is something you choose of your own free will. Ideas include attending an event you would not normally go to, wearing something you wouldn't normally wear, or switching a long-established routine or habit at work.

But what is it you have to work out for yourself? What is the nature of problems you encounter as a manager, leader or simply as a human being? There is no easy way to answer, of course, but try this mind-spinning thought for size – the hunt for self-improvement can be intense and long, but what if the reason you want to change is also the reason that you haven't? What if the only obstacle truly in your way is you? I like to tease Executive MBA groups with the thought that the *only* way anyone can find out that they never needed the MBA in the first place is by doing the MBA. That doesn't make the MBA a waste of time – far from it – but it does allow the graduate a lot of freedom to grow in ways they never expected at the start because they must shed their preconceived explanations and excuses.

Putting it together: a manifesto for lifelong leadership

In recent years, and as part of the MBA Personal Development course, I have been working with people from many fields and backgrounds to try and capture some of what we know about lifelong learning and leadership. The result is a short Reflective Leader's manifesto, an evolving series of affirmative statements to start walking by:

▌ I'm willing to recognise that my power as a leader or manager does not come from me, but through me.

▌ I strive for learning, not perfection (perfectionism is, by definition, unobtainable and meaningless). I know that there are many blind spots in my experience and knowledge. Therefore, I keep my humility, honouring the diversity of the wisdom of others. The alternative to perfectionism is awareness.

▌ Leaders have the power to transform and affect the world. I become a leader when I remind myself and others each day that the goal of collective transformation is a priority and more important than individual goals of personal success. True success is the success of the community.

▌ Judging others will not help them and will interfere in my ability to manage and lead. As a leader, I therefore seek awareness of my own emotions in every moment. This awareness puts the emphasis on my capacity to support others in transition. We all have fears, doubts and feelings that our weak areas are a liability (not necessarily). In our vulnerability lies our power for transformation.

▌ Keeping up-to-date in my knowledge and skills through inquiry and study is my obligation. It is not a choice, but a responsibility I have. I'm happy to revise my practice and assumptions every day. I'm happy to listen to others and, at the same time, I'm grounded in my values, convictions and beliefs.

TASK FOR CHANGE (4 OF 4)

Last one, and remembering to make notes as before, here is number 4 ...

Task 4

In the next three or four days, actively reach out and do something you have been avoiding or putting off.

This is, of course, a context-dependent offer. But it could be anything from experiencing going out to a restaurant just by yourself, to speaking to a person you have not spoken to for a long time or, for a strong reason, to getting to know a person you would never normally know, to deliberately engaging with people who have ideas you don't agree with.

When done, reflect on the tasks as a whole. What do you notice?

Personal development is about revealing, not changing, who you are. You already have everything you need; there's nothing to be fixed and nothing missing. As Roman Emperor and stoic philosopher Marcus Aurelius wrote in his notebooks: 'It never ceases to amaze me: we all love ourselves more than other people, but care more about their opinion than our own.' (Meditations, book 12).[3]

QUESTIONS FOR REFLECTION

1. Go back and look at your responses to the four activities in the introduction to Part 1. How has your perspective changed? Are there ways that you have changed your perspective? How are you better informed about your work or yourself?

2. Where do you go from here? What's your next step?

One final quotation to sum up the practical side of personal development, this time from the Chinese scholar Zhu Xi, 'Study extensively, inquire carefully, ponder thoroughly, sift clearly, and practice earnestly.'[4]

With that, I wish you every success in your career and in your journey of self-awareness as a manager.

Further reading

A classic text: *Tao Te Ching* by Lao Tzu (Stephen Mitchell's translation), a collection of ancient wisdom and poetry, in 81 verses (2015), Frances Lincoln.

Going deeper: *The Reflective Practitioner: How Professionals Think in Action* by Donald Schön (2010), Ashgate. From 1983, this has influenced many theorists while resisting temptation to turn itself into another two-by-two matrix or questionnaire.

Watch these: Short clip from a 2017 Charlie Rose interview with Bill Gates and Warren Buffet, which reveals Buffet's approach to time: **https://www.youtube.com/ watch?v=1ox93uTQds4**.

Also worth watching is the full interview: **https://www.youtube.com/ watch?v=OMu4ndH1iqs**.

'Trial, error and the God complex', a TED talk from 2011 by economist Tim Harford that asks us to choose a new mindset for our problems and puzzles: **www.ted.com/talks/tim_harford**.

Notes

1 Brook, P. (2008) *The Empty Space*, Penguin Modern Classics.
2 They almost certainly are not. A friendly reviewer of this chapter reminded me of the 'Spotlight effect', in which we tend to over-estimate how much people around us are aware of our world, when, in fact, they are convinced that we are absorbed in theirs.
3 Marcus Aurelius (2006), *Meditations*, Penguin Classics.
4 Zhu Xi, (1986), Zhuxi yulei, *Classified Dialogues of Master Zhu*, Li Jingde (ed.), Beijing: Zhonghua shuju.

Glossary

Selected terms used in MBA thinking

Much MBA vocabulary can be picked up from titles in the reading suggestions in *MBA Day by Day*. This list is more personal. Some of the entries have been used in this book while others are simply terms about learning that I believe every manager should know.

Artificial Intelligence (AI) No other technology trend is having (or is likely to have) the same effect on how we live and do business than the rapid developments in artificial intelligence, which may be defined as the computing capacity to perform functions usually requiring or signifying human intelligence. Once the province of science fiction, AI is entering mainstream business operations.

Assumption A frame of reference; a shortcut and basis for belief that is accepted by us and unnecessary to examine before we act. However, to learn, grow and change we must challenge our assumptions and examine those things we take for granted (see **Reflection**).

Behaviourism A branch and theory of psychology that is interested in observable, measurable actions rather than thoughts or mental constructs. Originally it was made popular in management by the work of John Watson and B.F. Skinner in the 1930s. Because management is seen as a matter of what managers do, this approach lives on in modified form (e.g. in the study of organisational behaviour).

Best practice   A current, structured and repeatable process that has proven successful (i.e. with a positive impact in terms of value). Best practice is always aligned to existing processes and systems and strategic intent. Over time, best practice is evaluated by others and can become a benchmark that other organisations can copy or adopt.

Blockchain   Capitalising on increased costs and a lack of trust in centralised control, a blockchain is a way to capture, store and share transactions that are time-stamped, secure and immutable by using the distributed nature of networked computing systems to replace a central institution of record. Although it rose to fame as the technology behind Bitcoin, its components had been around for many years. Still a young technology, evolving cases of its use are found across many industry segments.

Business model   Every organisation has a business model because every organisation is a collection of purposes, methods, norms, strategies, relationships and activities that keep it going. By default, whatever your organisation actually does – that is its business model. There is no shortage of academics, consultants and pundits to suggest new business models, however.

Coaching (executive)   It is fashionable now to expect managers to coach their subordinates. This is dangerous. A coaching mindset may be powerful, but power can cause conflict of interest or, worse, it can corrupt. The essence of coaching is to be of use to another person as they identify and work towards goals – on their terms, not yours. Coaching needs positive intent, genuine curiosity and insightful questions, as well as action.

Competency   Competencies are behaviours that you are judged to do well, or should do well. This has become the most popular way of thinking about what management is. Job descriptions are designed around the competencies that the post holder should exhibit, and performance appraisals usually measure results against a prescribed list of behaviours. The problem is that in different contexts different behaviours can prove highly destructive.

Emotional intelligence (EI)   Of interest to many, including occupational psychologists, EI has been popularised in the books of Daniel Goleman[1] but draws on the earlier work of Howard Gardner ('multiple intelligences').[2] EI is the attempt to measure how adept you are at monitoring yours and others' emotional states and to use this ability to guide behaviours. There is no general agreement as to whether these are learnable skills or innate traits, or both. Or neither.

Flow   In psychology, a description, developed by Hungarian–American psychologist Mihaly Csikszentmihalyi, of the state of being fully involved and engaged with what one is doing.[3] At work, flow is experienced when the level of challenge faced and level of skill available are both sufficiently advanced. It is often linked to moments or periods of high productivity by individuals or groups.

Game theory   A mathematical technique developed by John von Neumann to calculate the outcomes of conflicting situations among theoretical players of a game, all of whom are assumed to be rational and in possession of full information.[4] It has been applied to economics and to operational and strategic decision making but is a poor indicator of management decisions in open, social systems.

Heuristic   A heuristic is a way of working towards a solution to a problem through the use of an approximate series of trial and error. Heuristic thinking is intended to be fast and uses shortcuts, rules of thumb or educated guesses. However, if the underlying structure is not reflected in the rule of thumb, it can lead to serious error.

Human relations movement (HRM)   The HRM grew as a contrast
to the scientific movement (see **Technical rationality**) and
is an interdisciplinary approach to maximising productivity
that draws on social psychology and sociology. HRM
has become synonymous with the idea of employee
engagement and empowerment as essential to motivation,
but does not challenge the hierarchical status quo.

Inference   Reaching conclusions or questions based on
reasoning and logic. Three forms are most common:
1 **Induction,** which is moving from the particular
(observed) to the general (unobserved), only from
observation of a set of examples in the past. The
conclusion of an induction is always wider than its set
of premises. It is often the basis for heuristic (i.e. rule of
thumb) thinking; 2 **Deduction,** which is widely used in
theory building to form hypotheses to test (i.e. falsify)
a theory. Deduction starts with a premise, which is a
general statement of a covering rule, and moves to a
specific case (a hypothesis). If the covering rule is
correct, any conclusion deduced must logically follow
(e.g. if A = B and B = C, then A = C). If the conclusion
is false, then the premise must be incorrect and a better
covering rule needs to be determined; 3 **Abduction,** which
starts with a hunch, or an informed guess, to build the idea
behind a theory. Abduction means applying a rule or pattern
found elsewhere to explain the phenomenon puzzling you.

Information   Given how often managers go on about it, it is
surprising how rarely the word information is defined in
business. The common-sense definition might be 'data', but
there are many types of data that do not become information.
Information is news (to you) of a change or difference. Only
data that make a difference become information.

Internet of Things   Seen by some as best expression of the
third manifestation of the world wide web, the Internet of
Things (IoT) is where internet-enabled devices are set up

to communicate directly with one another. There is much business-to-business as well as business-to-consumer potential in the innovative use of this developing technology for pre-emptive control, monitoring and fault prevention. How autonomous, and how adaptable to Artificial Intelligence the IoT can become is an open and exciting question.

Knowledge management   The practical activity of capturing, storing and using information and data within an organisation and also the managerial activity of using this to create value. There are various interpretations of what this means, but they broadly divide between a focus on data storage and a focus on communicational exchange.

Lineal (vs circular) causation   A lineal relationship is one where a series of causes and effects in a sequence does not end back where it started. Lineal sequences can occur in closed systems. The opposite of lineal is recursive, which is the circular causality of feedback loops found in complex systems. Linear is a mathematical term for a relation between variables that can be plotted in a straight line. The opposite of linear is non-linear.

Mentoring   The process whereby a person with experience offers guidance and encouragement to someone younger or more junior. Mentors are expected to give advice and share their experience. Mentoring requires time, effort, trust and confidentiality on both sides and should be for a fixed duration. Mentoring is not coaching.

Paradigm (shift)   An over-used term in business and management, it was the subject of an influential book by Thomas Kuhn in 1962.[5] In science, a paradigm is the orthodox framework of ideas that members of a community can no longer legitimately dispute. These become, over time, the worldview. But science learns and when there is a change in what we all agree we know at a fundamental level, Kuhn calls this a paradigm shift.

Pareto principle   The 80/20 rule, and perhaps the most elegantly simple management principle in circulation. The heuristic that 80 per cent of one thing is often attributable to 20 per cent of another (e.g. when 80 per cent of your turnover comes from 20 per cent of your customers). Knowing this can help you direct your efforts to where they will have greatest impact.

Profit maximisation   The idea that it is a manager's duty to maximise short-term profits that seems to drive much decision making. This view is sometimes challenged and there are many counter-examples but in practice it still dominates much economic theory as well as popular conceptions of businesses and the people who run them.

Reductionism (vs holism)   Western science prizes intellectual activity that seeks the simplest, most economical explanation. This, however, may not be the only way of explaining the world around us and in fact may be counter-productive when taken to extremes. The counter-argument is that explanation may also come from seeing one context in terms of a larger whole.

Reflection   This definition is a good starting point: 'Reflection is a process, both individual and collaborative, involving experience and uncertainty. It is comprised of identifying questions and key elements of a matter that has emerged as significant, then taking one's thoughts into dialogue with oneself and with others.'[6]

Seminal   Any work, opinion or publication that strongly influenced others or appears transformed in later developments may be described as seminal, or formative. Seminal works are those that you should go back to in order to understand and decode those later works, which may have taken ideas as given (see **Assumption**).

Technical rationality   The view that management consists of the solving of practical problems through the application of scientific theory and method. Specialist technical knowledge is what sets the manager apart from the non-manager, a view championed in the period between the two world wars and, though things have changed, many organisations still value a rigorous, systematic and standardised application of professional knowledge.

Notes

1 Goleman, D. (1996) *Emotional Intelligence: Why it Can Matter More Than IQ*, Bloomsbury Publishing.
2 Gardner, H. (2006) *Multiple Intelligences: New Horizons in Theory and Practice*, 2nd edition, Basic Books.
3 Csikszentmihalyi, M. (2002) *Flow: The Psychology of Happiness: The Classic Work on How to Achieve Happiness*, Rider.
4 von Neumann, J. and Morgenstern, O. (2007) *Theory of Games and Economic Behavior*, 60th Anniversary Commemorative edition, Princeton University Press.
5 Kuhn, T. (2012) *The Structure of Scientific Revolutions*, 50th anniversary edition, University of Chicago Press.
6 Jay, J.K. and Johnson, K.L. (2002) 'Capturing complexity: A typology of reflective practice for teacher education', *Teaching and Teacher Education*, 18(1): 73–85.

Index

Page numbers in **bold** relate to glossary entries;
Page numbers followed by *f* indicate figures;
those followed by *t* indicate tables.